# Cambridge
# Poetry
# Workshop

16+

Jeffrey and Lynn Wood

CAMBRIDGE
UNIVERSITY PRESS

PUBLISHED BY THE PRESS SYNDICATE OF THE UNIVERSITY OF CAMBRIDGE
The Pitt Building, Trumpington Street, Cambridge CB2 1RP, United Kingdom

CAMBRIDGE UNIVERSITY PRESS
The Edinburgh Building, Cambridge CB2 2RU, United Kingdom
40 West 20th Street, New York, NY 10011-4211, USA
10 Stamford Road, Oakleigh, Melbourne 3166, Australia

First published 1998

Printed in the United Kingdom at the University Press, Cambridge

Typeset in Optima and Meridien Roman

*A catalogue record for this book is available from the British Library*

ISBN 0 521 57472 2 paperback

CORNWALL COLLEGE
STUDY CENTRE

Prepared for publication by Paren & Stacey Editorial Consultants
Designed and formatted by Geoffrey Wadsley
Picture research by Jane Taylor

Cover photograph of *LesTrès Riches Heures de Jean, Duc de Berry* © Faksimile Verlag, Luzern, Switerland

# Introduction

*Cambridge Poetry Workshop 16+* is designed to help teachers integrate the teaching of verse into their everyday explorations of English in use. Throughout, the emphasis is as much upon the processes of listening and speaking and writing imaginatively as on responding to the verse in a discretely critical fashion. We hope that teachers will now discover some new and productive ways of stimulating students to work collaboratively and individually on tasks which are intrinsically rewarding. These tasks are also suitable for different kinds of assessment.

It will be apparent to people familiar with our other anthologies that in this book we pay more attention to speaking and listening activities. We have made more explicit the stages by which the preliminary engagement with topic and theme can lead to a wide range of performance and writing activities and then back to oral work of different kinds. Arguably, Listening and Speaking are the most important skills students need to develop. However, curiously little guidance has been given to teachers about how listening skills might be promoted. Yet if there is one thing which distinguishes most poetry from most prose, it is surely that verse is intended to be heard rather than seen. Students often find poetry unappealing because it is presented to them as something to read with their eyes rather than with their ears.

We hope that whenever there is time, teachers will see preparing readings of the poems (by themselves or by their pupils) as something to address first. Students should encounter poetry as living sound, not as dead, cold print. In our experience, students who hear a poem, not just once but many times as the work on it develops, respond imaginatively with a confidence and enthusiasm which the daunting sight of the text on the page rarely promotes.

In each unit we offer a range of assignments. Teachers will adjust these to fit their schemes of work. Few groups will tackle every task with every poem. We hope you will find that many of the activities will work well with other texts.

And sometimes no follow-up work may be appropriate. Even in our assessment-driven climate, listening to poetry does not always need the justification of a designated outcome. The Workshop functions at one level as an anthology of wonderful literature, much of which students rarely encounter. If this book does no more than introduce people to Achilles, Gawain and the Green Knight and Falstaff, it will have performed a valuable service.

Cambridge 1998                                    Jeffrey & Lynn Wood

For Tom

# Hints on using the book

We have grouped the poems into six broad categories. However, each unit is complete in itself. Our intention is to enable teachers to use the book flexibly, moving freely from one unit to another to suit their schemes of work.

### To Begin at the Beginning
These units introduce students to some pre-16th century writing, to stimulate interest in the ways the language and the craft of poetry have evolved and to help students to see how the preoccupations and oddities of characters from the remote past are surprisingly familiar.

### Voices
The most fascinating challenge to anyone involved in creative writing is to give very different characters ways of speaking which reveal their personalities without obtrusive commentary from their authors. The pieces in this section attempt to do just that. The reader has the illusion that s/he is encountering people who 'give themselves away'. The samples invite students to challenge simplistic distinctions between spoken and written English, between the language of art and the language of the streets. In the process students bump into some celebrated literary creations who might not otherwise have crossed their path.

### The Theatre of the Imagination
The central piece here is Shakespeare's apology for poetic drama: a practical exploration of the ways in which the 'meaning' of any work of literature involves the active participation of the reader with the text. The units introduce notions of indeterminacy explored more fully in the units with which the book concludes.

### Cityscape
Voices from different cultures respond to a common theme, initiating a debate which students are encouraged to develop. This unit is designed to promote confidence and competence in the skills of the comparison of texts.

### Return Journey
The poetry of Carol Ann Duffy speaks with provocative directness to young people's experience of growing up. All of these units are designed to stimulate students' personal writing, to facilitate discussion of the changes that are happening in their own lives and to help them articulate their personal insights into how far anyone's past 'contains' their future.

### Re-presentations
These exercises in deconstruction, pastiche, parody and imaginative extension involve students in critical and creative investigations which will help prepare them for the study of Language and Literature at Advanced level.

# Contents

# The Poets

| | |
|---|---|
| The Iliad | probably written down about 750 BC |
| Gawain and the Green Knight | probably written about 1375 |
| Blacksmiths | probably written about 1450 |

| | |
|---|---|
| Chaucer | 1343-1400 |
| Marlowe | 1564-1593 |
| Ralegh | 1554-1618 |
| Shakespeare | 1564-1616 |
| Wordsworth | 1770-1850 |
| Byron | 1788-1824 |
| Browning | 1812-1889 |
| George Eliot | 1819-1880 |
| Hopkins | 1844-1889 |
| Newbolt | 1862-1938 |
| Kipling | 1865-1936 |
| Manmohan Ghose | 1869-1924 |
| Alfred Douglas | 1870-1945 |
| T S Eliot | 1888-1965 |
| C Day Lewis | 1904-1972 |
| Dylan Thomas | 1914-1953 |
| Christopher Logue | born 1926 |
| Ted Hughes | born 1930 |
| Jenny Joseph | born 1932 |
| Andrei Voznesensky | born 1933 |
| Seamus Heaney | born 1939 |
| Angela Carter | 1940-1992 |
| Ian McEwan | born 1948 |
| Carol Ann Duffy | born 1955 |
| David Green | born 1965 |

*Anon* | BLACKSMITHS

## THINKING/TALKING POINTS

In groups: thirty minutes

- How do you imagine 'Neighbours from Hell'?

  Talk about the relative pain of finding yourself living near each of the following. Think of the various things which would drive you mad.
  Jo's Car Body Repairs
  Ritz Academy of Tap Dancing
  Kwik Kebab
  East Cheape Bell Foundry
  Mega Screen 2000
  The Revivalist Meeting-House
  Athena's Organic Pig Farm
  Bert's Jazz Club
  Maxwell's Abattoir/Renderer
  A.A.A. Minicabs
  Bird World
  Trotter Taxidermy

- Give each neighbour a rating, one to ten. Ten is 'Hell'.
  Justify your rank-order to the other groups. Then negotiate an agreed scale of anguish. You may like to display your results in the style of a tourist's guide.

## PERFORMANCE

In groups: one hour

- Someone, somewhere in the Middle Ages, driven wild by the relentless crash-bashing next door, turned torment into the noisiest poem in English.

  Experiment with ways of performing it.

- Look through it silently a few times. Then work on the poem together. Each take a line. Practise saying it aloud. Then read the poem around the group. Keep it moving – don't stop to correct stumbles.

- When you've done this a few times, try out different ways of saying/shouting/chanting/singing the piece. For example, you could read some lines more than once; you could use several voices for some bits, single voices for the rest.

- You have a choice of how to pronounce some of the words. For example, do you prefer 'knavene' (line 4) pronounced like the modern word 'knee' (with 'k' silent), or more like the Welsh place-name 'Caernarfon'? Try out the endings of words too. Do you think 'dintes' (line 2) sounds best as one syllable or two: 'dints' or 'dint-ez'? If a word ends with an 'e', you may like it best with an extra syllable. For example, 'cammede' (line 5) could be pronounced 'cammeda'.

Don't worry what the words mean. Enjoy the sounds and the movement and the fury as the speaker, for the fifth night in a row, can't get a wink of sleep. The blacksmiths are working overtime.

- You may like to tape your performances.

# Blacksmiths

Swarte-smeked smethes, smatered with smoke,
Drive me to deth with den of here dintes:
Swich nois on nightes ne herd men never,
What knavene cry and clatering of knockes!
The cammede kongons cryen after 'Col! col!'
And blowen here bellewes that all here brain brestes.
'Huf, puf,' seith that on, 'Haf, paf,' that other.
They spitten and sprawlen and spellen many spelles,
They gnawen and gnacchen, they grones togidere,
And holden hem hote with here hard hamers.
Of a bole hide ben here barm-felles,
Here shankes ben shakeled for the fere-flunderes.
Hevy hameres they han that hard ben handled,
Stark strokes they striken on a steled stocke.
Lus, bus, las, das, rowten by rowe.
Swiche dolful a dreme the Devil it to drive!
The maister longeth a litil and lasheth a lesse,
Twineth hem twein and toucheth a treble.
Tik, tak, hic, hac, tiket, taket, tik, tak,
Lus, bus, lus, das. Swich lif they leden,
Alle clothemeres, Christ hem give sorwe!
May no man for brenwateres on night han his rest.

## ASSIGNMENT

◆ Examining 'Blacksmiths'
a) Pick out what you think are the ten noisiest words in the poem.
b) Which words suggest physical effort?

Choose a dozen words or phrases from the poem which are unknown to you. Have a guess at what each one means. Perhaps some don't have a meaning but are just imitations of all the different noises the blacksmiths make.

Think about what makes this writing 'poetic'. Can you see or hear any tricks the writer uses to hold the poem together?

◆ Making your own poem
Now write your own lyric. Let off steam about your obnoxious neighbour(s). Try to model your poem on 'Blacksmiths'. Use twenty-two lines and see if you can write it with four stressed syllables in every line, as there are here:

**Swart**e-smeked **smeth**es, **smat**ered with **smok**e,
**Drive** me to **deth** with **den** of here **dint**es ...

What else do you notice about these two lines? You'll hear that one thing missing is rhyme. If you make your poem rhyme it won't sound much like 'Blacksmiths'. Feel free to invent words to imitate whatever is so irritating about the people next door: noises, smells, movements, glare, the atmosphere of the place.

One student invented these words. She was describing the nasty smells wafting from a brewery: gooeyloges, schmuklestinks, pongery, pisstunkfroth, sprooter, psmitchifunk.

Illustrate your poem and make a class display of 'Neighbours from Hell'. You may like to record your poems onto tape with linking narrative, sound effects or music. You could put your recording into the library or onto the school's website so others can enjoy your misery.

*from SIR GAWAIN AND THE GREEN KNIGHT*

**Setting the Scene**

The place is Camelot, the court of King Arthur and Queen Guenevere; the time, New Year's Day, many centuries ago. It is like a scene in a tapestry. The loveliest ladies imaginable; handsome, brave knights whose manners are as gentle as their arms are strong, and a King and Queen loved and admired by all. Everyone is in the prime of life.

By day there has been jousting. Mass has been sung in chapel. It is now night time and everyone is dressed in their finery, feasting and dancing, exchanging gifts, playing games and singing, celebrating Christmas, and the New Year's arrival. The banqueting hall, adorned with exquisite silk hangings, is filled with light, the glitter of jewels, the music of trumpets, pipes and kettledrums, the sound of laughter and a never-ending stream of rich food served on sparkling silver dishes. Young Queen Guenevere, fabulously dressed, sits in the place of honour, under a richly embroidered canopy decorated with gems.

The youthful King is restless with excitement, anxious that everyone else should be served first. Full of life, he will not eat until he has heard a new story of adventure and mystery or watched a joust.

Abruptly the music stops. There's a great commotion. From nowhere, a huge and handsome horseman bursts into the hall. He wears no armour and carries no weapons except, in his left hand, a mighty axe, sharp as a razor. His appearance mesmerises everyone. From head to foot, he is as vibrantly green as a Christmas tree in winter. Long flowing locks of green hair, a great bushy green beard, a good-looking green face, powerful green hands. His elegant clothes are green too: his tunic embroidered with birds and butterflies, his ermine fur-lined cloak, his broad belt studded with green gems, his splendid enamelled golden spurs. Even his mighty horse is green. Its mane is plaited with gold and green thread, its splendid saddle and all its elegant trappings are set with jewels. Everything is as intensely green as the hollybush the huge horseman carries in his right hand, a sign of peace.

The whole court is stunned. They have seen many marvels but nothing like this. In the tense silence, the Green Knight addresses the King.

**The Challenge**

The Green Knight tells Arthur he has come to Camelot to find out if the knights of the Round Table are as brave and as honourable as everyone says. But he's not proposing a joust: none of the youngsters he sees around him could possibly fight such a mighty warrior as he! No, what he has in mind is a game, some Christmas fun. Who dares to play? It's a very simple game. The challenger will take the mighty axe and strike a blow upon the Green Knight. But he must agree to let the Green Knight return that blow in a year and a day's time.

Everyone is rooted to the spot. Silent. Arthur's brave knights look anywhere but at the green giant. He mocks their cowardice. Goaded, young King Arthur jumps to his feet and accepts the strange challenge. The Green Knight dismounts and hands him the axe.

Just as the King prepares to strike the first blow, his young nephew, Sir Gawain, steps forward. He begs Arthur and everyone present to let him try. It is more fitting that someone insignificant, the weakest and least of the company, should take the foolish risk rather than the King himself.

Gawain's request is granted. Giving him God's blessing, Arthur hands over the huge axe to the brave young man. Gawain promises faithfully to keep the bargain. He will strike the blow then, in a year and a day's time, all alone, hunt out the Green Knight, wherever he lives, and submit to the return blow.

**The Beheading**

The giant Green Knight kneels and bows his head. He sweeps his lustrous long hair from his neck. He does not flinch. Gawain lets the great axe fall under its own weight, slicing the Knight's head clean from his body. Shocked, the onlookers shove the head away from them with their feet.

Then the impossible happens. Sturdily, the headless knight walks over to where his lovely head has rolled. He picks it by the hair and mounts his mighty green horse. Speaking just as before, he reminds Gawain of the bargain they have made. He will be waiting for Gawain next New Year's Day at the Green Chapel. Then, as mysteriously as he came, the Green Knight gallops away, fire flashing as his horse's hooves strike the flints. Leaving everyone in the hall dumbstruck.

## THINKING/TALKING POINTS

• Talk about the story and how it affected you. Have you ever heard anything like it?

## FIRST ASSIGNMENT: WORKING ON THE MANUSCRIPT

In small groups, and in pairs

◆ You have read a modern retelling of the beginning of one of the oldest English poems. It was written about 1370 in the dialect of Cheshire and

The grene knyȝt vpon grounde graybely hym dresses,
A littel lut with þe hede, þe lere he discouerez;
his longe louelych lokkez he layd ouer his croun,
Let þe naked nec to þe note schewe.
Gauan gripped to his ax and gederes hit on hyȝt,
Þe kay fot on þe folde he be-fore sette,
Let hit doun lyȝtly lyȝt on þe naked,
Þat þe scharp of þe schalk schyndered þe bones,
and schrank þurȝ þe schyire grece, and schade hit in twynne,
Þat þe bit of þe broun stel bot on þe grounde.
Þe fayre hede fro þe halce hit to þe erþe,
þat fele hit foyned wyth her fete, þere hit forth roled;
þe blod brayed fro þe body, þat blykked on þe grene.

Lancashire. Opposite is what a few lines of the original version of the poem look like.

In the extract below, R T Jones has kept all the original words, but used our modern alphabet. Here is the moment when Gawain strikes off the Green Knight's head:

> The grene knight upon grounde graithely him dresses,
> A littel lut with the hed, the lere he discoveres,
> His long lovelich lokkes he laid over his croun,
> Let the naked nek to the note shewe.
> Gawain gripped to his axe, and gederes hit on hight;
> The kay fote on the folde he before sette,
> Let hit doun lightly light on the naked,
> That the sharp of the shalk shindered the bones
> And shrank thurgh the shire grece, and shadde hit in twinne,
> That the bit of the broun stel bot on the grounde.
> The fair hed fro the hals hit to the erthe,
> That fele hit foined with her fete, there hit forth roled.
> The blod braid fro the body, that blikked on the grene;
> And nauther faltered ne fel the freke never the helder,
> Bot stithly he start forth upon stif shankes,
> And runishly he raght out, there as renkes stoden,
> Laght to his lufly hed, and lift hit up sone,
> And sithen bowes to his blonk; the bridel he caches,
> Steppes into stelbawe and strides aloft,
> And his hed by the here in his hand holdes;
> And as sadly the segg him in his sadel sette
> As non unhap had him ailed, thagh hedles he were in stedde.
> He braide his bulk aboute,
> That ugly body that bledde;
> Mony one of him had doute,
> By that his resouns were redde.

Imagine that this fragment of *Sir Gawain and the Green Knight* has been discovered between the pages of an old Bible found preserved in a medieval tomb. No-one is very sure what all the words mean. The story is well-known but there is no complete dictionary of this particular English dialect.

You are the team working on the manuscript, trying to turn it into lively modern English. If you speak the words aloud and ignore the spelling, some of the language is almost the same as it would be today:

> Gawain gripped ... his axe ...
> ... the bridel he caches ...
> And his hed by the here in his hand holdes ...
> That ugly body that bledde ...

Other phrases are fairly easy to understand:

> His long lovelich lokkes he laid over his croun ...
> The blod braid fro the body ...

Some bits you could probably make a guess at:

> ... shindered the bones ...
> And shrank thurgh the shire grece ...
> The fair hed fro the hals hit to the erthe,

Some of the language is more mysterious. Many of the words can be found in the dialect dictionary below. For the rest, it is up to you to experiment, seeing what makes the best sense, what you think sounds best. Divide up the extract amongst the group, each pair working on a sentence or two.

Begin by reading your section through a few times aloud. How much of the sense is obvious? Use the dictionary to help you with any tricky bits.

See if you can keep some of the sounds of the original in your version.

## DIALECT DICTIONARY

You may want to use a modern dictionary and/or a thesaurus as well to find words which have similar meanings to the definitions we have given but which you think will sound better in your translation.

**ailed:** troubled
**bit:** blade, cutting edge
**blikked:** shone, gleamed
**blonk:** horse, steed, charger
**bot:** bit, cut into
**braid:** spilled, spurted, burst
**braide:** twisted, turned
**broun:** bright, shining
**bulk:** trunk, headless body
**croun:** top, crown of the head
**discoveres:** uncovers, reveals

**doute:** fear
**fele:** many people, folk
**foined:** kicked, spurned
**folde:** ground
**freke:** man, knight
**gederes:** lift with both hands (together)
**graithely:** at once, immediately
**hals:** neck
**him dresses:** takes up his position, stance, stand
**hit:** it

**in stedde:** instead
**kay:** left
**laght:** seized
**lere:** flesh
**lut with:** bent, bowed
**raght:** reached
**redde:** declared
**renkes:** knights, men
**resouns:** speech
**runishly:** roughly, fiercely
**sadly:** steadily, firmly
**segg:** fellow, man, knight

**shalk:** man, fellow, knight
**shankes:** legs
**sharp:** sharp blade
**shire grece:** fair, white flesh
**sithen:** next, afterwards, then
**sone:** at once, quickly
**stelbawe:** stirrup
**stithly:** stoutly, undismayed
**the helder:** the more for that
**to the note:** *either* in readiness *or* to the nape, the part where the short hairs grow

## PLENARY

- Listen to what each group has produced and discuss how successfully you have managed to re-present the episode in exciting modern English. Discuss the sections you think need revision. Redraft the whole episode, working together.

- When you have made a version of the whole extract that you are pleased with, you may like to make a large copy for display, perhaps using medieval lettering and decorating it like an illuminated manuscript. You could even bake it in an oven to make it look old.

## SECOND ASSIGNMENT: DEVELOPING A FILM SCRIPT

*In small groups: two hours*

◆ Imagine that you have been commissioned to produce a script for a new film of *Sir Gawain and the Green Knight* for television. It is to be broadcast during the Christmas holidays.

Discuss whether you will present the piece for a family audience, for adults or for children. Talk about how the audience you have in mind will influence the way you re-present the story. Discuss the advantages and disadvantages of the various ways the story might be presented, for example, as an animation, as a play, as a reading interspersed with still pictures.

Reread the section called 'The Challenge' a couple of times; then plan how you will turn it into a filmscript.

This will involve giving the King, Gawain, some of the courtiers, and perhaps the Green Knight as well, their lines to speak, developing what the extract gives as *reported speech* into *direct speech*. Note that in the extract the reported speech gives only a brief summary of what is actually said:

> He begs Arthur and everyone present to let him try. It is more fitting ...

In developing your script, try to give the audience a strong sense of each character's personality and mood from the way s/he talks. Think about different tones of voice and the different kinds of vocabulary each might use. How will you convey each character's reaction to the challenge – through their body language, and the rhythm and tempo of what they say?

Set your final draft out as a film script, complete with instructions to the camera operator, lighting department, sound effects team and to the actors (or animators) about how the various characters should look and move. If you haven't seen one, you will probably find it helps to look in the library at the filmscript of a work you know well.

Here are some of the abbreviations used in a screenplay:

| CAM | camera | EVE | evening |
|-----|--------|-----|---------|
| V/O | voice-over | Cont. | continued |
| EXT | exterior | INT | interior |
| CU | close-up | ECU | extreme close-up |
| POV | point of view | | |

## FOR FURTHER STUDY

There are many modern versions of the old poem. These are some of the best:

Selina Hastings: *Sir Gawain and the Green Knight* (Walker Books)
Theodore Howard Banks Jr: *Gawain and the Green Knight* (Appleton Century Crofts, New York)
R T Jones: *Sir Gawain and the Greene Gome* (Heinemann)
Marie Borroff: *Sir Gawain and the Green Knight* (Longman)
J R R Tolkien: *Sir Gawain and the Green Knight, Pearl, Sir Orfeo* (George, Allen and Unwin)
Ian Serraillier: *The Challenge of the Green Knight* (Oxford University Press)
W R J Barron: *Sir Gawain and the Green Knight* (Manchester University Press) – original text and modern prose version

# *Chaucer* | THE WEDDING NIGHT

## THINKING/TALKING POINTS

You are going to read or listen to an intimate account of what happened on a couple's wedding night.

- Jot down some of your expectations about what you'll read or hear. How do you picture the husband? And the wife? What do you think each of them might be thinking and feeling as they get into bed together?

- Talk about what each of you has written. What are the most interesting similarities and differences between what each of you expected?

- In order to write the story yourself, what further information do you think is needed:
  a) about the man?
  b) about the woman?
  c) about their relationship?
  d) about their backgrounds?
  e) about when and where the story takes place?
  f) about anything else?

## FIRST ASSIGNMENT

*In pairs: one hour*

◆ Brainstorm some ideas around the following scenario:
The action begins just before the couple get into bed and ends the next morning. The man in the story is called January. He is rich. He is sixty. All his life he's had women whenever he liked. Suddenly he has decided it's time he got married. The woman is called May. She is about seventeen. The story is set in Pavia, in Italy, in the fourteenth century.

◆ You have to decide how to present the scene and the couple. Here are some things you might like to think about:
  – why a very old man might wish to marry a young girl
  – why a young girl might wish to marry a very old man
  – the most likely outcome of such a marriage.

◆ Write an extract from a story or a play based on the scenario above. Your extract is called 'The Wedding Night'.

Here is Chaucer's version of what you have written. It comes from *The Merchant's Tale*. The wedding celebrations over, the guests leave and the couple are alone.

| | |
|---|---|
| **Parfourned … ark diurne:** The sun had completed its daily journey | Parfourned hath the sonne his ark diurne; |
| **sojurne:** remain | No lenger may the body of him sojurne |
| **th'orisonte:** the West | On th'orisonte, as in that latitude. |
| **derk:** dark | Night with his mantel, that is derk and rude, |
| **rude:** harsh | Gan oversprede the hemisperie aboute; |
| **this lusty route:** all these jolly guests | For which departed is this lusty route |
| **lustily:** eagerly | Fro Januarie, with thank on every side. |
| **leste:** wished | Hoom to hir houses lustily they ride, |
| | Where as they doon hir thinges as hem leste, |
| | And whan they sye hir time, goon to reste. |
| **hastif:** impatient | Soone after that, this hastif Januarie |
| | Wolde go to bedde; he wolde no lenger tarye. |
| **ypocras:** an aphrodisiac | He drinketh ypocras, clarree, and vernage |
| **clarree … vernage:** sweet wines | Of spices hoote, t'encreessen his corage; |
| **corage:** performance | And many a letuarie hath he ful fyn, |
| **letuarie:** remedy | Swiche as the cursed monk, daun Constantin, |
| **daun Constantin… *De Coitu:*** a sexual guide written in the 11th century by Constantine Afer | Hath writen in his book *De Coitu*; |
| | To eten hem alle he nas no thing eschu. |
| **nas … eschu:** leave nothing out | And to his privee freendes thus seyde he: |
| | 'For Goddes love, as soone as it may be, |
| | Lat voiden al this hous in curteys wise.' |
| | And they han doon right as he wol devise. |
| **travers:** curtains around the bed | Men drinken and the travers drawe anon. |
| **abedde:** to bed | The bride was broght abedde as stille as stoon; |
| | And whan the bed was with the preest yblessed, |
| **every wight:** everybody | Out of the chambre hath every wight him dressed; |
| | And Januarie hath faste in armes take |
| **make:** mate, partner | His fresshe May, his paradis, his make. |
| | He lulleth hire, he kisseth hire ful ofte; |
| | With thikke brustles of his berd unsofte, |
| | Lyk to the skin of houndfissh, sharp as brere – |
| | For he was shave al newe in his manere – |
| | He rubbeth hire aboute hir tendre face, |
| | And seyde thus, 'Allas, I moot trespace |

To yow, my spouse, and yow greetly offende,
Er time come that I wil doun descende.
But nathelees, considereth this,' quod he,
'Ther nis no werkman, whatsoevere he be,
That may bothe werke wel and hastily;
This wol be doon at leyser parfitly.
It is no fors how longe that we pleye;
In trewe wedlok coupled be we tweye;
And blessed be the yok that we been inne,
For in oure actes we mowe do no sinne.
A man may do no sinne with his wyf,
Ne hurte himselven with his owene knyf;

**leve:** permission

For we han leve to pleye us by the lawe.'
Thus laboureth he til that the day gan dawe;

**a sop:** a piece of bread

And thanne he taketh a sop in fyn clarree,
And upright in his bed thanne sitteth he,
And after that he sang ful loude and cleere,
And kiste his wif, and made wantown cheere.

**made wantown cheere:** celebrated wildly

**coltissh:** lively as a young horse

**ragerye:** passion

**a flekked pye:** a spotted magpie

**craketh:** croaked

He was al coltissh, ful of ragerye,
And ful of jargon as a flekked pye.
The slakke skin aboute his nekke shaketh.
Whil that he sang, so chaunteth he and craketh.
But God woot what that May thoughte in hir herte,
Whan she him saugh up sittinge in his sherte,
In his night-cappe, and with his nekke lene;

**nat ... worth a bene:** worthless, pathetic, useless, hopeless

She preyseth nat his pleying worth a bene.

### THINKING/TALKING POINTS

Look through the points which follow. Then read the passage once again before talking about them.

- Suggest some of your own words to describe January, or draw your own cartoon of him. Now do the same thing for May. Compare your results and discuss the way each of you imagines the couple.

- 'May is described in a particular way at the beginning of the passage. At the end she comes across very differently. We've all been taken in.' Do you agree with this comment? Was the way you imagined May or felt about her any different the second time you heard the piece? Why?

- What about January? Did your feelings about him alter when you reread the passage? Why?

- Pick out six details which you find particularly dramatic, exciting, shocking, funny, disgusting, disturbing or memorable in any way. What exactly does each one make you imagine and feel? See if you can explain how the details achieve their effect. Is it the images which make them striking? Is it the sounds of the words? Is it the way the rhymes emphasise certain details?

### PERFORMANCE

- Read the passage once again to yourself.

  What tone of voice do you think each stage of the story should be read in: serious, comic, tender, crude, sarcastic, loving? Where do you think you should raise or lower your voice? Where should you slow down or speed up?

- Now in pairs or groups of four, prepare a performance of the passage. Take a sentence or section each. Don't worry about how you pronounce the words. Keep the lines moving steadily.

### SECOND ASSIGNMENT

Two hours: choose one

◆ May's Story
Imagine you are May. The following day, while your husband sleeps, you send your dearest friend a letter telling her everything about your sudden marriage. Last week you were chosen by January, the rich old

knight, to be his bride and you agreed. Why? What were your feelings about January then? What were your motives?

Describe in some detail, the wedding, the wedding night, your thoughts about your husband and what you look forward to now. Do you feel proud, ashamed, excited, smug, in love? Or are you regretting it?

Think carefully about the character of May. Choose a style of writing you think will best bring out her personality.

◆ A critical essay
Write a close critical study of all the ways Chaucer brings this scene to life.

What impression of a) January, and b) his 'fresshe May' do you think the storyteller wishes to give us? How does he go about it?

Refer closely to at least a dozen details from the text in your essay. Remember to talk about not just what the words mean, but what they sound like and what they make you see and feel.

Does the passage give you any impression of the storyteller? What sort of person do you think s/he is? Why?

# Homer | from *THE ILIAD*
# Christopher Logue | from *WAR MUSIC*

Here is a version of the opening of one of the oldest stories ever written down. Many of the episodes in the tale had probably been circulating a long time amongst storytellers before they were put together and turned into a book about 800 B.C.

## From *The Iliad*

This tense opening episode takes place on the windswept plains separating the sea and the mighty walled city of Troy. A huge army raised by all the famous warrior kings of Greece, under the leadership of Agamemnon and Menaleus, has been camped there for many years, laying siege to the city. Their aim is to raze Troy to the ground. Menaleus's beautiful wife, Helen, has been abducted by the Trojan Prince Paris. The Trojans must pay. Despite many battles between the two great armies, nothing decisive has been achieved. In the Greek camp, there is friction, rivalry and bad blood between the generals.

O goddess, tell us about Achilles' anger. Anger that caused the Greeks such grief. Anger that sent many a brave soul hurtling to hell; that fed many heroes to dogs and vultures. Thus were the orders of Jove fulfilled from the day when Agamemnon, King of Kings, and the mighty warrior Achilles first fell out.

And which of the gods fired their quarrel? Apollo it was. Apollo who, furious with the king, sent a pestilence to plague the people. Because King Agamemnon had dishonoured Apollo's priest Chryses.

Begging for his daughter's release, and bringing with him a huge ransom, Chryses had approached the Greek ships. In his hands he carried the sceptre of Apollo bound with a suppliant's wreath. And he pleaded with the Greeks. But most of all with their two commanders.

'Agamemnon and Menaleus, sons of Atreus,' he cried, 'and all other Greeks! May the gods of Olympus grant you sack Priam's city and reach your homes safely. But set free my daughter. Accept this ransom for her, in reverence to Apollo, son of Jove.'

With one voice, the Greeks were moved by his petition. All but Agamemnon, who spoke fiercely. 'Old man, let me not find you loitering here by our ships. Neither your sceptre nor your wreath impress me. Your daughter remains mine. She shall grow old far from her own home, in my house at Argos, working at her weaving and visiting my bed. Leave now. Do not provoke me or it will be the worse for you!'

Fearful, the old man obeyed. Silently he took himself away to the shore where the sea pounded. Alone he prayed to Apollo. 'Hearken to my grief,' he cried, 'God of the silver bow. If ever I have honoured you with rich sacrifices, listen to my pleas. Let your arrows avenge these father's tears upon the Greeks!'

Apollo heeded his prayer. Furious, he flew down from Olympus, his bow and his quiver upon his shoulder. The arrows rattled on his back as he trembled with rage, his face dark as night. Apollo's silver bow dealt deadly arrows into the midst of the Greeks.

First he slaughtered their mules and their hounds. Presently he targeted the people themselves. All day long the stench rose from the burning pyres of the dead.

For nine whole days, Apollo's arrows fell upon the Greeks. Upon the tenth, great Achilles summoned an assembly. Moved by the suffering of her people, the goddess Juno urged Achilles, her favourite, to act. Now he rose to speak.

'Agamemnon,' he began, 'To escape destruction, we should take to our ships and make for home. Here war and pestilence decimate us. We must ask some priest, some seer, some prophet, some reader of the dreams sent by the gods to discover what angers Apollo. Whether we have broken some vow, denied some sacrifice and offended him. Enquire what we must do to appease him.'

Calchas, the reader of signs, the master who knew what was past and what was to come, rose to speak. Long ago. he had guided the Greeks to the Trojan shore.

With sincerity he addressed them. 'Great Achilles, you ask me to reveal the cause of Apollo's fury. I will do so. But first I beg your protection. A plain man cannot withstand the anger of a King.'

Achilles answered. 'Speak out, fearlessly. As long I live no Greek shall lay hands upon you. Not Agamemnon himself.'

Then the seer spoke boldly. 'Apollo is angry for the sake of his priest. Agamemnon has dishonoured him. We have been punished and will be punished further yet unless Chryses's daughter is restored. Without ransom. And sacrifices made to the God.'

As the seer sat down, Agamemnon rose, his heart black with rage, his eyes flashing fire. 'Seer of evil, not once have you predicted any good to me. Your prophesies are a catalogue of calamities. And now you perform your tricks here amongst the Greeks, claiming Apollo plagues us because I would not take a ransom for this girl, the daughter of Chryses. The girl I love better than Clytemnestra, my wife, whose equal she is in beauty, in wit and accomplishments. Yet, surrender her I will if I must; I would have the people live, not die. But you must find me a prize in her place, or I alone among the Greeks shall be without one.'

Achilles answered, 'Most noble son of Atreus.

'Grasping, greedy beyond all mankind! How shall we find you another prize? We have no storehouse of prizes. Those we took from the cities have been awarded; we cannot take them back. Give up this girl, therefore, to the God. And if ever Jove grants us to sack the city of Troy we will repay you richly. Three and four times over.'

Agamemnon answered. 'Achilles, no matter how brave you are, you must know your place! Shall you keep your prize, while I sit tamely and surrender mine on your instructions? Let the Greeks find me a girl in fair exchange to my liking, or I will come and take yours or that of Ajax or of Ulysses. And there will be no negotiating.

'But, we will deal with this later. For the present, let us draw a ship into the sea, load a sacrificial offering, free Chryseis and put her aboard to appease Apollo's anger.'

Scowling, Achilles lashed back. 'Underhanded, boastful, grasping Agamemnon! Why should Greeks risk death daily for you? I have no grudge against the Trojans I fight. We followed you, the King of Contempt, for the sake of your honour, not ours. To punish the Trojans for the slur on your house. And how do you repay us? By threatening to rob me of the prize for which I have toiled and bled in battle, my tribute from the soldiers.

'Whenever the Greeks conquer rich Trojan cities, yours is the grandest reward! No matter that I endure most, achieve most in battle. I shall return to my kingdom, not wear myself out here heaping up treasures for trash.'

And Agamemnon answered, 'Suit yourself. Scurry back home! I'll not stand in your way. Others here respect me. Above all Jove himself. No king here is so vile as Achilles! Always dissatisfied! Always quarrelling! A rabble-rousing traitor! Your bravery is a god's gift. Why should you be so proud? Pack your baggage! Sail home to lord it over your Myrmidons. I care neither for your soldiership nor for your tantrums. But I've made up my mind. Since Apollo demands Chryseis from me, I shall come to your tent and take pretty Briseis, your prize. To show the world who leads the Greeks. To show the world the cost of cocky disobedience.'

Achilles was livid with fury. His hand hovered over the hilt of his sword. Within his seething breast his heart was divided. Should he push the others aside and skewer the son of Atreus, or check his rising anger? While he was thus in two minds, was just beginning to draw his huge sword from its scabbard, Minerva came down from heaven seizing the great Achilles by his golden hair. He turned in amazement to see the goddess invisible to everyone's sight but his. He knew her at once by her brilliant eyes. 'Why are you here,' said he, 'daughter of great Jove? To watch arrogant Agamemnon pay for his insolence with his life?'

But Minerva said, 'I come from heaven to curb your anger. Juno has sent me, who loves both her Achilles and her Agamemnon. Cease brawling. Lift your fingers from your sword. Rage at him if you will. I promise you this. Your gifts will be three times as splendid for suffering this insult. Hold, therefore, and obey.'

'Goddess,' answered Achilles, 'however angry a man may be, he must respect your commands.'

And so Achilles stayed his hand on the silver hilt of his sword. But his wild words rang out. 'Wretched drunken lout,' he cried, 'with the face of a dog and the spirit of a frightened rabbit. Too cowardly to lead an army into battle! You shun fighting as you shun death itself. Instead you sneak about filching prizes from greater men who stand up to your insolence. You lord it over feeble folk.

'Now hear this loud and clear. Surely and solemnly do I swear this before all the Greeks. Hereafter they shall seek Achilles and shall not find him. In the day of your distress, your despair, your desperation, when men fall dying in heaps under the murderous blows of mighty Trojan Hector, you, Great Agamemnon, shall not know how to help them. Then you will rend your heart with rage for the hour when you dared insult the bravest of the Greeks.'

## THINKING/TALKING POINTS

When you have listened to or read the passage a couple of times, discuss the following points.

- What sort of story is it? How is it like/unlike:
  a) a soap opera   b) a fairy tale   c) a Bible story   d) a thriller
  e) an historical drama?

- What kind of world/universe do you think the story takes place in? How is it like/unlike the one you live in?

- What kind of language do the narrator and the people in the story use? How is it like/unlike everyday speech? Talk about any films you've seen in which characters speak in a similar way.

- This scene is about Achilles's anger which has dreadful consequences later in the story. See if you can explain exactly what made Achilles mad. How far do you sympathise with him? Why?

- Do you think the storyteller admires any of the people in the story?

Look through the extract again and pick out some words and phrases to help you decide.

- Who do you think is the most powerful character in the story? Why?

- What do you notice about the way the women in this story are presented?

- Talk about the ways in which you think this story might develop.

## FIRST ASSIGNMENT

**Choose one**

Reread the story again a couple of times.

◆ Choose a moment from the story, or a particular character to illustrate. Use a picture style which you think suits the style of writing. You may wish to use some words from the text as captions or to weave them into the design of your picture.

Make a display of the different pictures people produce and talk about what you think works well in each one.

◆ Imagine yourself as Chryseis, Briseis or as one of Achilles's soldiers, reflecting on what has happened. Write a diary entry in which you record what occurred on this fateful day and explore your feelings about the people involved, especially Achilles and Agamemnon. Add lots of imaginative details. For example, you may like to describe where the scene took place and what these larger-than-life characters looked like.

Decide whether to write your piece in the present or in the past tense and be careful to keep to it all the way through.

◆ In groups, experiment with ways in which this famous scene could be acted. You may structure your script/improvisation around the conversations here but feel free to use your own words and alter/add some incidents. You may wish to change some details to suit your particular audience.

Talk about how you will give the audience some idea of the various characters' power and importance. What do you think will be the best way of showing that not all the characters in this episode are human?

# From War Music (Patrocleia)

The Plains of Troy. Some months later...

Now hear this:
While they fought around the ship from Thessaly,
Patroclus came crying to the Greek.

'Why tears, Patroclus?' Achilles said.
'Why hang about my ankles like a child
Pestering its mother, wanting to be picked up,
Expecting her to stop what she is at, and,
In the end, getting its way through snivels?
    You have bad news from home?
Someone is dead, Patroclus? Your father? Mine?
But news like that is never confidential.
If such was true, you, me, and all the Myrmidons
Would cry together.
    It's the Greeks, Patroclus, isn't it?
You weep because a dozen Greeks lie dead beside their ships.
But did you weep when those same Greeks condoned my wrongs?
If I remember rightly, you said – nothing.'

    And Patroclus:
'Save your hate, Achilles. It will keep.
Our cause is sick enough without your grudging it my tears.
    You know Odysseus is wounded?
Orontes, too – his thigh: King Agamemnon, even. Yet
Still you ask, *why tears?*
    Is there to be no finish to your grudge?
No, no; don't shrug me off. Mind who it is that asks:
Not the smart Ithacan; not Agamemnon. Me.
And God forbid I share the niceness of a man,
Who, when his friends go down, sits tight
And finds his vindication in their pain.
    They are dying, Achilles. Dying like flies.
Think, if you cannot think of them, of those
Who will come after them; what they will say:
    *Achilles the Resentful* – can you hear it? –
Achilles, strong? ... *The Strongest of the Strong* –
And just as well, because his sense of wrong was heavy.
    Shameful that I can talk to you this way.'

All still.

'And yet, among the many who do not,
As I believe that God and She who bore
You to a mortal husband backs your claim,
So I believe They will not censor mine:

Let me go out and help the Greeks, Achilles.
Let me command your troops. Part of them, then?
And let me wear your armour.'

Still.

'Man – it will be enough!
Me, dressed as you, pointing the Myrmidons ...
The sight alone will make Troy pause, and say:
"It's him," a second look will check them, turn them,
Give the Greeks a rest (although war has no rest) and turned,
Nothing will stop us till they squat behind their Wall.'

And so he begged for death.

'Better to ask yourself,' Achilles said,
'If you would stay my friend or not
Than speculate which God, or whether God Himself,
Packaged the specious quibbles with my mouth
Your insolence delivers to my face.

Why not add Agamemnon to your whine?
King vain, king fretful, truthless Agamemnon,
Eager to eat tomorrow's fame today.

Go on ... *He was a sick man at the time, Achilles.*
*He did it to avoid unpleasantness, Achilles.*
*Achilles, he was not-too-well advised.'*

Staring each other down until he said:
'O love,
I am so glutted with resentment that I ache.

Tell me, have I got it wrong?
Did he not take the girl I won?
Did none of my fair-weather friends agree
That she was mine by right of rape and conquest? Yet,
When it comes to it, they side with him; the royal slug
Who robs the man on whom his crown depends.

Yet done is done; I cannot grudge forever.
Take what you want: men, armour, cars, the lot.'

Easy to see his loss was on the run;
Him standing, saying:
'Muster the troops and thrust them, hard,

Just here' – marking the sand – 'between the enemy
And the Fleet.
Aie! ... they are impudent, these Trojans ...
They stroke our ships,
Fondle their slim black necks, and split them, yes –
Agamemnon's itchy digits make me absent,
My absence makes them brave, and so, Patroclus,
Dear Agamemnon's grab-all/loose-all flows.
    All right: if not Achilles, then his vicar.
Forget the spear. Take this' – one half its length – 'instead.
You say Odysseus is out? Bad. Bad. And Ajax, too?
No wonder all I hear is
Hector, Hector, Hector, everywhere Hector,
As if he were a God split into sixty!
    Hurry, Patroclus, or they will burn us out ...
But listen first, Hard listening? Good.
    Hear what I want:
My rights, and my apologies. No less.
And that is all.
    I want the Greeks saved, yes;
Thereafter – Agamemnon at my tent,
With her, Briseis, willing, at my feet;
And many gifts.  Be clear about the gifts.
    And one thing more before you go:
Don't overreach yourself, Patroclus.
Without me you are something, but not much.
Let Hector be. He's mine – God willing.
In any case he'd make a meal of you,
And I don't want you killed.
But neither do I want to see you shine
At my expense.
    So mark my word:
No matter how, how much, how often, or how easily you win,
Once you have forced the Trojans back, you stop.
    There is a certain brightness in the air,
Meaning the Lord Apollo is too close
For you to disobey me and be safe.
You know Apollo loves the Trojans; and you know
That even God our Father hesitates
To contradict Apollo ...
    O friend,
I would be glad if all the Greeks lay dead
While you and I demolished Troy alone.'

## THINKING/TALKING POINTS

When you have read or listened to the passage two or three times, discuss the following points.

- How is the way this part of the story is told similar to/different from the way the opening was told? Describe this storyteller's tone of voice and the kind of language he uses. Discuss the way Patroclus and Achilles speak to one another. Do you think this narrator respects the people in the story? Why?

  Look through the text and pick out twenty words and phrases which help you decide.

- What impression of Achilles does this passage give you?
  And of Patroclus?

- What do you think might happen in the next stage of the poem?

## SECOND ASSIGNMENT

Choose one: two hours

◆ Read the opening of the story again. You will find it on page 22.

Choose three or four sentences which you think are exciting or important. See if you can rewrite them in a style similar to the one Christopher Logue used in his version.

Write a commentary on your work, explaining what features of Christopher Logue's style you were trying to imitate and assessing how successful you think you have been. Quote from your version and from the extracts from Logue and the prose version in your commentary to illustrate the points you are making.

◆ Choose a passage from *War Music* to re-present in your own way.

You may like to rewrite it in a style similar to the one used for the opening. You may wish to present it in a different idiom: say, in the kind of language you think a class of fifteen-year olds would enjoy. You could deliberately mix styles, new and old, epic and casual, colloquial and formal, as in Baz Luhrmann's film of *Romeo and Juliet*.

You may prefer to re-present it as a storyboard, using some of Christopher Logue's language as captions.

◆ Re-present this episode as if you are Patroclus describing what led up to this conversation and then how you felt trying to reason with your mighty friend, Achilles.

Add lots of descriptive details of your own to what we're given in Christopher Logue's version. Try to convey something of Patroclus's mixed and changing feelings.

You may like to continue the story, describing what happened when Patroclus put on Achilles's armour and led his troops into battle.

## FOR FURTHER STUDY

There have been many retellings of *The Iliad*, Homer's story of the siege and destruction of Troy. Some of them have been in prose, others in various styles of verse. To some extent, each age 'rediscovers' Homer and re-presents the tales in a style which reflects the world in which the latest storyteller lives.

Here are a few translations you may like to dip into, for the pleasure of reading or hearing them, to compare for their differences in tone, diction, imagery and form, and for differences in their attitude to the story.

George Chapman (1611); Alexander Pope (1715-1720); Lord Derby (1865); Samuel Butler (1898-1900); A T Murray (1924); E V Rieu (1950) [now recorded on Penguin Audio Cassettes by Derek Jacobi on ISBN 0140 860053]; Richmond Lattimore (1965-7); Christopher Logue as 'War Music', 'Kings' and 'The Husbands' (1981, 1991, 1994)

# *T S Eliot* | from *THE WASTELAND*

T S Eliot's poem *The Wasteland* was published in 1922. When it came out, it disturbed people who expected poetry to be written as it had been in the past. They were puzzled by the poem because of its fragmented way of presenting things.

Today we're used to this technique. It is how most films and television programmes work. We no longer expect to be given a continuous story set in one location at a particular time. We're used to reading narratives in which there are abrupt shifts in time and place. We're comfortable with the idea of several things happening simultaneously. This style of story-telling reflects our everyday experience of living, which is more like a patchwork than a still-life.

In *The Wasteland*, Eliot paints a picture of modern life, mostly through scraps of conversation between all sorts of people. Although there may be more than one person *talking*, this doesn't always develop into *conversation*.

Eliot presents these scraps of monologue and dialogue without any comment and with few narrative links. The poem is more like a collage, or a series of impressions than a story which has a beginning, a middle and an end. *The Wasteland* could be described as 'a play for voices'.

## THINKING/TALKING POINTS

Thirty minutes

- What do you imagine when you hear the word 'wasteland'?
  Describe some images the word conjures up for you.

- Discuss some popular films and television programmes where the audience has to keep track of lots of different things happening in different places at different times without any explanatory links.

- What's the difference between two people talking together and two people having a conversation? Describe an experience you've had of a non-conversation.

- Before you explore some extracts from the poem, discuss why you think

Eliot chose to present most of his speakers as anonymous. What does that suggest about what living in *The Wasteland* is like?

## PERFORMANCE

In pairs: one hour

Here are some extracts from *The Wasteland*.

- Work through these fragments a few times, taking turns to read.

  Try reading each extract in different sorts of voices (young/old, tired/excited, quick/slow, high/low) until you're happy with a particular voice for each fragment.

  In some cases you will probably wish to give a fragment to one voice. Others will work better if you divide them between you.

  Don't worry about anything you don't understand. Often we get a strong impression of someone's mood and personality even though we're not sure what they're talking about. Think how television advertisements sometimes present people speaking in languages few viewers understand.

- Polish your performances until you're ready to present them to the rest of the class.

(i)

April is the cruellest month, breeding
Lilacs out of the dead land, mixing
Memory and desire, stirring
Dull roots with spring rain.
Winter kept us warm, covering
Earth in forgetful snow, feeding
A little life with dried tubers.

(ii)

Summer surprised us, coming over the Starnbergersee
With a shower of rain; we stopped in the colonnade,
And went on in sunlight, into the Hofgarten,
And drank coffee, and talked for an hour.
Bin gar keine Russin, stamm' aus Litauen, echt deutsch.
And when we were children, staying at the arch-duke's,
My cousin's, he took me out on a sled,
And I was frightened. He said, Marie,
Marie, hold on tight. And down we went.

In the mountains, there you feel free.
I read, much of the night, and go south in the winter.

### (iii)

    Madame Sosostris, famous clairvoyante,
Had a bad cold, nevertheless
Is known to be the wisest woman in Europe,
With a wicked pack of cards. 'Here,'said she,
'Is your card, the drowned Phoenician Sailor,'
(Those are pearls that were his eyes. Look!)
'Here is Belladonna, the Lady of the Rocks,
The lady of situations.
Here is the man with three staves, and here the Wheel,
And here is the one-eyed merchant, and this card,
Which is blank, is something he carries on his back,
Which I am forbidden to see. I do not find
The Hanged Man. Fear death by water.
I see crowds of people, walking round in a ring.
Thank you. If you see dear Mrs. Equitone,
Tell her I bring the horoscope myself:
One must be so careful these days.'

### (iv)

    'My nerves are bad to-night. Yes, bad. Stay with me.
Speak to me. Why do you never speak? Speak.
    What are you thinking of? What thinking? What?
I never know what you are thinking. Think.'

    I think we are in rats' alley
Where the dead men lost their bones.

'What is that noise?'
                    The wind under the door.
'What is that noise now? What is the wind doing?'
                    Nothing again nothing.

            'Do
You know nothing? Do you see nothing? Do you remember
Nothing?'

                I remember
Those are pearls that were his eyes.

'Are you alive, or not? Is there nothing in your head?'

But

0 0 0 0 that Shakespeherian Rag

It's so elegant

So intelligent.

'What shall I do now? What shall I do?

I shall rush out as I am, and walk the street

With my hair down, so. What shall we do tomorrow?

What shall we ever do?'

The hot water at ten.

And if it rains, a closed car at four.

And we shall play a game of chess,

Pressing lidless eyes and waiting for a knock upon the door.

### (v)

When Lil's husband got demobbed, I said –

I didn't mince my words, I said to her myself,

HURRY UP PLEASE IT'S TIME

Now Albert's coming back, make yourself a bit smart.

He'll want to know what you done with that money he gave you

To get yourself some teeth. He did, I was there.

You have them all out, Lil, and get a nice set,

He said, I swear, I can't bear to look at you.

And no more can't I, I said, and think of poor Albert,

He's been in the army four years, he wants a good time,

And if you don't give it him, there's others will, I said.

Oh is there? she said. Something o'that, I said.

Then I'll know who to thank, she said, and give me a straight look.

HURRY UP PLEASE IT'S TIME

If you don't like it you can get on with it, I said.

Others can pick and choose if you can't.

But if Albert makes off, it won't be for lack of telling.

You ought to be ashamed, I said, to look so antique.

(And her only thirty-one.)

I can't help it, she said, pulling a long face,

It's them pills I took, to bring it off, she said

(She's had five already, and nearly died of young George.)

The chemist said it would be all right, but I've never been the same

You *are* a proper fool, I said

Well, if Albert won't leave you alone, there it is, I said,

What you get married for if you don't want children?

HURRY UP PLEASE IT'S TIME

Well, that Sunday Albert was home, they had a hot gammon,

And they asked me in to dinner, to get the beauty of it hot –
HURRY UP PLEASE IT'S TIME.
HURRY UP PLEASE IT'S TIME.
Goonight Bill, Goonight Lou. Goonight May. Goonight.
Ta ta. Goonight. Goonight.
Good night, ladies, good night, sweet ladies, good night, good night.

(vi)

Weialala leia
Wallala leialala

'Trams and dusty trees,
Highbury bore me. Richmond and Kew
Undid me. By Richmond I raised my knees
Supine on the floor of a narrow canoe.'

'My feet are at Moorgate and my heart
Under my feet. After the event
He wept. He promised 'a new start'.
I made no comment. What should I resent?'

'On Margate Sands.
I can connect
Nothing with nothing.
The broken fingernails of dirty hands.'

## PLENARY

One hour

- Discuss the ways each of you developed your performances. Did each of you 'hear' the same sorts of characters? Can some snippets be performed convincingly in lots of different ways?

- Discuss your impressions of the various speakers. What tricks did Eliot use to create those impressions? Which characters seem to have trouble communicating?

Here are some things to look at:
  – diction: the sorts of words each speaker uses
  – the rhythm and the tempo of his/her words
  – the way each fragment is punctuated
  – the different tones of voice you heard.

- What sorts of lives do you think these different people lead? What were you able to work out about their pasts, and their present situations? How would you present each one on film?

- Do you feel these inhabitants of *The Wasteland* have anything in common with each other? Why?

- Which of the speakers do you most/least admire or pity? Why?

- Taken together, what impression of *The Wasteland* does Eliot convey to you through these fragments?

- What do you think the title *The Wasteland* means? Literally and metaphorically? Do you think the world you live in is at all like this? Why?

# Dylan Thomas | from *UNDER MILK WOOD*

The idea of writing a 'play for voices' has been experimented with many times since Eliot wrote *The Wasteland*. A powerful – and very different work – written for BBC radio is Dylan Thomas's *Under Milk Wood*.

We learn about the characters in *Under Milk Wood* through their conversations, dreams, fantasies and confessions. They are the inhabitants of an imaginary Welsh village, Llareggub, a place of claustrophobic morality, hypocrisy and rebellious energy. You might like to think about what the name of the place suggests. Try reading it backwards.

Here is an extract from *Under Milk Wood*. Read it through a few times.

MRS OGMORE-PRITCHARD
Mr Ogmore!
Mr Pritchard!
It is time to inhale your balsam.

MR OGMORE
Oh, Mrs Ogmore!

MR PRITCHARD
Oh Mrs Pritchard!

MRS OGMORE-PRITCHARD
Soon it will be time to get up.
Tell me your tasks, in order.

MR OGMORE
I must put my pyjamas in the drawer marked pyjamas.

MR PRITCHARD
I must take my cold bath which is good for me.

MR OGMORE
I must wear my flannel band to ward off sciatica.

MR PRITCHARD
I must dress behind the curtain and put on my apron.

MR OGMORE
I must blow my nose.

MRS OGMORE-PRITCHARD
In the garden, if you please.

MR OGMORE
In a piece of tissue-paper which I afterwards burn.

MR PRITCHARD
I must take my salts which are nature's friend.

MR OGMORE
I must boil the drinking water because of germs.

MR PRITCHARD
I must make my herb tea which is free from tannin.

MR OGMORE
And have a charcoal biscuit which is good for me.

MR PRITCHARD
I may smoke one pipe of asthma mixture.

MRS OGMORE-PRITCHARD
In the woodshed, if you please.

MR PRITCHARD
And dust the parlour and spray the canary.

MR OGMORE
I must put on rubber gloves and search the peke for fleas.

MR PRITCHARD
I must dust the blinds and then I must raise them.

MRS OGMORE-PRITCHARD
And before you let the sun in, mind it wipes its shoes.

## THINKING/TALKING POINTS

• What do you learn about the personalities of these three speakers in this brief exchange?

## ASSIGNMENT: WRITING A PLAY FOR VOICES

**Two hours**

◆ Everyone has his/her favourite words and phrases. Close your eyes and imagine these people:
- – your mother, father or carer
- – one of your neighbours
- – your best friend
- – your head teacher

Listen to their voices in your head.

Are there certain expressions peculiar to each of them? How would each of them answer the telephone? What would each one say if they hadn't seen you for a while? What would they say if the weather were bad? If they were asking you a favour or telling you off? For example, would any of them use any of these words or phrases:

| | |
|---|---|
| Like I say | That's well out of order |
| So what happen man? | I were really scared |
| I won't tell you again | Chance would be a fine thing |
| You are a pet | I don't suppose by any chance |
| Doolally | Are yis with me? |
| It'll all turn out right in the end | Mustn't complain |
| You'll die when I tell you | She was pissing herself |
| My heart was in my boots | Just a jiffy |
| It's just not on | Well I never! |
| Fingers crossed | Stay cool, my man |
| I believe you're mistaken | I'm not one to complain but … |
| Sick as a parrot | Sussed her out straight off |
| Right! | Hubby |
| Use a bit of common | Dinnae ken |
| It takes all sorts | The Wife's Mother |
| Good thinking | Everything's under control. |

Now think about real and imaginary characters in films, on television and in books you've read. Choose half a dozen and see how many of their favourite expressions and catch-phrases you can recall.

Have a go at writing your own scenes for voices. Choose a particular group of people to focus on. It could be:
a) a family
b) your street or village

c) your school or college
d) a club
e) the primary school you once attended.

The setting could be a place where lots of different people unexpectedly find themselves jumbled together. For example:
a) a supermarket
b) the scene of an accident
c) in a railway train stuck at a signal
d) in a bus queue
e) at a package holiday camp site
f) in an old people's home.

Forget about plot. Nothing much should 'happen'. The piece is intended to give the audience fleeting impressions of a group of people: their personalities, their similarities, their differences. It should also give some sense of the particular world they share: its values, expectations, atmosphere and flavour.

Experiment with ways of giving people of different ages and different backgrounds distinctive things to talk about and distinctive ways of speaking.

Some voices may sound posher than others. Some may sound more, some less, lively. It's the variety of voices which matters: pompous, gloomy, chirpy, philosophical, couldn't-care-less, polite, coarse, edgy, brash ...

Experiment with *diction, punctuation, rhythm* and *tone* to make each speaker come across as an individual. Remember, it's not so much what people say as the way that they say it which matters.

## FOR FURTHER STUDY: COMPARING PLAYS FOR VOICES

Dylan Thomas was in the BBC cast which broadcast a powerful play for voices by David Jones. *In Parenthesis* is a complex narrative interspersed with fragments of dialogue. It explores the changing experience of war through the ages. Scenes set in the foul trenches of the 1914–18 War intermingle with episodes from wars in ancient mythology. Dylan Thomas was probably inspired by David Jones's play to produce his much more light-hearted piece *Under Milk Wood*.

You can listen to the original BBC broadcasts of both plays. They have been reissued on audio cassette in the *Burton at the BBC* anthology.

# Browning | *MY LAST DUCHESS*

Few nineteenth century plays are still performed today. The most successful forms of imaginative writing were poetry and the novel.

See how many names of nineteenth-century playwrights, poets and novelists you can come up with. Describe any nineteenth-century work of fiction you know well. What do you most enjoy about it? How is it most/ least like the best film you've seen in the last year?

One kind of poem which was developed particularly by the mid-century poets Tennyson and Browning was the dramatic monologue. A *dramatic monologue* is similar to a soliloquy from a play, except that there is no play. What we learn in the speech is all that we learn: about the story, about the situation and about the character. As with characters in plays, the best dramatic monologues reveal personalities quite distinct from that of the poet who created them. Although they are written in the first person, we pick up quickly if the speaker is not trustworthy or likeable. The speaker may not realise what s/he is revealing about him/herself!

Most of Browning's dramatic monologues are spoken by real or imaginary characters from the period of the Italian Renaissance. Painters, musicians, bishops and dukes come forward and tell us the truth about themselves, or try to.

Listen to or read through the following dramatic monologue a few times. What impression of the speaker does it give you?

(Note: we have adjusted the paragraphing here to make the stages in the poem easier to recognise. As in most soliloquies, it's frequently the pauses, the silences which are most dramatic.)

# My Last Duchess

Ferrara

That's my last Duchess painted on the wall,
Looking as if she were alive. I call
That piece a wonder, now: Frà Pandolf's hands
Worked busily a day, and there she stands.
Will't please you sit and look at her?

I said
'Frà Pandolf' by design, for never read
**countenance:** face      Strangers like you that pictured countenance,
**earnest:** intense      The depth and passion of its earnest glance,
**puts by:** opens      But to myself they turned (since none puts by
The curtain I have drawn for you, but I)
**durst:** dared to      And seemed as they would ask me, if they durst,
How such a glance came there; so, not the first
Are you to turn and ask thus.

Sir, 'twas not
Her husband's presence only, called that spot
Of joy into the Duchess' cheek: perhaps
**mantle:** cloak      Frà Pandolf chanced to say 'Her mantle laps
Over my lady's wrist too much,' or 'Paint
Must never hope to reproduce the faint
'Half-flush that dies along her throat,' such stuff
**courtesy:** polite chat      Was courtesy, she thought, and cause enough
For calling up that spot of joy.
She had
A heart – how shall I say? – too soon made glad,
Too easily impressed, she liked whate'er
She looked on

and her looks went everywhere.

**favour:** present, probably      Sir, 'twas all one! My favour at her breast,
a brooch      The dropping of the daylight in the West,
The bough of cherries some officious fool
Broke in the orchard for her, the white mule
She rode with round the terrace – all and each
Would draw from her alike the approving speech,

Or blush, at least.

　　　　　　She thanked men – good! but thanked
Somehow – I know not how – as if she ranked
My gift of a nine-hundred-years-old name
With anybody's gift.

　　　　　　　　Who'd stoop to blame
This sort of trifling?
　　　　　　　　　Even had you skill
In speech – (which I have not) – to make your will
Quite clear to such an one, and say: 'Just this
Or that in you disgusts me;

　　　　　　　　　　here you miss,
'Or there exceed the mark' – and if she let
Herself be lessoned so, nor plainly set
Her wits to yours, forsooth, and made excuse,
- E'en then would be some stooping,

　　　　　　　　　　and I choose
Never to stoop.

　　　　　　　Oh sir, she smiled, no doubt,
Whene'er I passed her, but who passed without
Much the same smile?

　　　　　　　　　　This grew;

　　　　　　　　I gave commands;

Then all smiles stopped together.

　　　　　　　　　There she stands
As if alive.

　　　　　　Will't please you rise?  We'll meet
The company below, then.
　　　　　　　　　　I repeat,
The Count your master's known munificence
Is ample warrant that no just pretence
Of mine for dowry will be disallowed;

**lessoned:** taught a lesson

**munificence:** generosity
**pretence:** claim

**avowed:** made clear

Though his fair daughter's self, as I avowed
At starting, is my object.
                                    Nay, we'll go
Together down, sir.

                              Notice Neptune, though,
Taming a sea-horse, thought a rarity,
Which Claus of Innsbruck cast in bronze for me!

## THINKING/TALKING POINTS

- Discuss your first impressions of the speaker. Jot down a few adjectives to describe him.

- What do you think happened to the speaker's last wife?

- At the end of the poem, the speaker and his guest are about to go and meet somebody. Who? What business is about to be done?

Now read through the poem again, each taking a sentence in turn.

- What's your impression of the last Duchess? Pick out five or six details which you think bring her to life.

- What was it about the Duchess's behaviour which upset the Duke?

- What do you think the Duke's feelings are about the painting of the Duchess? What does this suggest to you about his personality?

- Do you think Browning expects us to find the Duke sympathetic? Why? (Note: When you're writing about characters in literature, the word 'sympathetic' means 'likeable', 'understandable' or 'admirable', not someone who feels pity.)

## ASSIGNMENT

**Choose one**

◆ Imagine you are Frà Pandolph, sent by the Duke to paint the girl about to become the next Duchess of Ferrara. Write a dramatic monologue in which the painter, between brush strokes, warns his subject about what may be in store for her. See if you can model your poem on the style of Browning's.

◆ Imagine yourself as the new Duchess. Record in a series of diary entries:

- your initial impression of the Duke and his palace
- your conversation with your father the night before the wedding
- the marriage ceremony
- your first impressions of life as the Duchess of Ferrara
- your discovery, behind the curtain, of the portrait of the Last Duchess
- your growing anxieties about your husband.

◆ Browning wrote another poem, unconnected with this one, called 'The Flight of the Duchess'. Imagine yourself as the Duchess who has realised what her husband is planning to do to her. Write a poem or a short story in which you explore her hopes and fears and her plans to escape before the thunderbolt falls.

## FOR FURTHER STUDY: COMPARING DRAMATIC MONOLOGUES

Here are the titles of some other dramatic monologues which you might like to explore, compare and/or imitate.

Tennyson: 'Ulysses'; 'Tithonus'
(You will find study units on these two monologues in *Cambridge Poetry Workshop GCSE*.)
Browning: 'Frà Lippo Lippi'; 'Andrea del Sarto'; 'The Bishop Orders His Tomb'; 'Caliban Upon Setebos'; 'Porphyria's Lover'; 'Any Wife to Any Husband'; 'The Last Ride Together'
T S Eliot: 'The Love Song of J. Alfred Prufrock'; 'Portrait of a Lady'; 'Gerontion'
Sylvia Plath: 'The Surgeon at Two a.m.'; 'Mirror'; 'Mushrooms'; 'Tulips'; 'Lesbos'; 'Daddy'
Ted Hughes: 'Hawk Roosting'; 'Soliloquy'; 'Cleopatra to the Asp'
Thom Gunn: 'The Unsettled Motorcyclist's Vision of his Death'; 'Human Condition'
Simon Armitage: 'Ten Pence Story'; 'Judge Chutney's Final Summary'; 'Lines Thought to Have Been Written on the Eve of the Execution of a Warrant for His Arrest'

# *Marlowe*  |  from *DR FAUSTUS*

## PRELIMINARY STUDY: WHAT IS A SOLILOQUY?

**One hour**

Unlike novelists who can fill in the background, scriptwriters must make their characters reveal themselves through what they do and say, and the way in which they behave. Other characters in the play may tell us things about them. But we can never be certain that what others say is the whole truth. This means that there may be moments when scriptwriters break the normal rules of theatre or film. If a character is hiding her/his true feelings from everyone else, or is in a situation where there's no one else to talk to, how can the audience find out what's going on in her/his mind?

In a novel, the narrator regularly fills in the missing links between conversations. We may be given a glimpse of a character's private letters or diaries. In a play, a device called a *soliloquy* allows the playwright to let the audience in on a character's innermost thoughts and feelings.

Describe to each other any soliloquies you know. How do they work to shape the way the audience feels about the speaker? For example, you may know a soliloquy which begins, 'To be or not to be ...'. What does that speech do to shape the way we feel about the speaker, even if we can't remember many of the words he says? What sort of person are we being told that speaker is?

A soliloquy is an artificial device. In real life, people don't speak their secret thoughts aloud, even when they're going mad. If they did, what came out wouldn't make much sense to anyone else. A skilled dramatist gives us the impression of someone speaking in a passion or a fit of depression. But to do the job well, s/he has to be in complete control of the material.

Film directors sometimes use 'voice-overs' so that we can be let in on a character's private thinking. In the theatre, a soliloquy often works best if it appears that the character is sharing ideas with the audience rather than talking to thin air. But if the situation is one where being utterly alone in a crisis is seen as exciting, we rely on the power of the actor to suspend the audience's disbelief.

In this unit, and the one which follows, we examine soliloquies from plays written about four hundred years ago.

# Introducing Dr Faustus

In his play about Dr Faustus, the man who struck a disastrous bargain with the Devil, Marlowe introduces us to his hero through a narrator. He gives us a potted history of Faustus's life up to the point where the action starts:

> Now is he born, his parents base of stock,
> In Germany, within a town called Rhodes:
> Of riper years to Wittenberg he went,
> Whereas his kinsmen chiefly brought him up.
> So soon he profits in divinity,
>
> ...
>
> That shortly he was graced with doctor's name,
> Excelling all, whose sweet delight disputes
> In heavenly matters of theology.
> Till, swollen with cunning, of a self conceit,
> His waxen wings did mount above his reach,
> And, melting heavens conspired his overthrow.
> For falling to a devilish exercise,
> And glutted more with learning's golden gifts,
> He surfeits upon cursed necromancy:
> Nothing so sweet as magic is to him,
> Which he prefers before his chiefest bliss.
> And this the man that in his study sits.

**Wittenberg:** a famous German university

**conspired:** plotted

**necromancy:** black magic

## EXPLORING THE TEXT

- Jot down in your own words the important things the narrator has told us about Faustus.

- Faustus has acquired much more knowledge than most of us ever could. But still he's not satisfied. As he puts it:

  Yet art thou still but Faustus, and a man ...

  Explain what you think he means by that.

- Faustus believes that the 'practice of Magic and concealed arts' will raise him above ordinary scholars. Driven by this insane ambition, Faustus calls up Mephistophilis, the Devil's agent. He makes the following bargain:

(I, Faustus) say, he surrenders up to him his soul
So he will spare him four and twenty years,
Letting him live in all voluptuousness,
Having thee ever to attend on me,
To give me whatsoever I shall ask ...
And always be obedient ...
Had I as many souls as there be stars
I'd give them all for Mephistophilis
By him I'll be great emperor of the world ...

**voluptuousness:**
luxury, sexual delight

Imagine writing a new version of this story. How would you re-present the deal Faustus makes, for a modern audience?

- When this play was written, four hundred years ago, the writer wanted to show that he was talking about a situation we could all be in. Hell is described in traditional, gruesome language at the end of the play. The pictures he paints are hideous:

    Now Faustus, let thine eyes with horror stare
    Into that vast perpetual torture-house.
    There are the Furies tossing damned souls,
    On burning forks; there, bodies boil in lead.
    There are live quarters broiling on the coals,
    That ne'er can die! This ever-burning chair
    Is for o'er-tortured souls to rest them in.
    These, that are fed with sops of flaming fire,
    Were gluttons, and loved only delicates,
    And laughed to see the poor starve at their gates ...

But earlier in the play, comes Mephistophilis's most chilling sentence. Asked how he comes to be out of Hell, wandering about the earth, his reply to Faustus is shocking:

    Why this is hell, nor am I out of it.

Talk about what you think this sentence means.

## THINKING/TALKING POINTS

- The story of Faust is known all over the world, it has been retold in many different ways. What films you've seen or stories you've read does it remind you of? How did the bargains in those versions of the story turn out?

- If you were given the chance to have everything you wanted, would you take it? Might there be any disadvantages?

- Talk about whether you think we are all potential Fausts. Is someone who takes drugs, or drinks and drives, for example, a kind of Faustus? Or somebody who deliberately marries a person s/he does not love?

## FIRST ASSIGNMENT

Two hours

◆ You are fifty. Twenty-four years ago, you negotiated away your soul. You've been given exactly what you asked for. Look about you: everything your heart desired has been delivered. In an hour, you have to settle accounts. Mephistophilis (or whoever) is coming to collect.

Have a go at writing a soliloquy in which you face the horrible consequences. You sealed the contract. Suicide's not an option. You committed yourself to Mephistophilis and his gang. To do with as they liked. For Eternity.

Write your soliloquy: the final speech of the play. Write in verse or prose, sharing your feelings with the audience. Maybe you'll touch on some of these things:
- how you feel about what you've achieved. What's been good, not so good about what you desired.
- how you imagine what's in store for you. Does the word 'Hellfire' conjure up any particular images? Are you beginning to understand where you will be in a few minutes' time? How that makes you feel as the final minutes tick away on that Rolex.
- what you think now about your younger self – and about Mephistophilis and his methods.
- how you fool yourself that you might escape, delay things a bit.
- how you face the fact that there's absolutely no way out.

In real time, the action lasts from eleven pm to midnight. On stage, your piece should take about five minutes to perform.

# Faustus's final soliloquy

## DEVELOPING A PERFORMANCE: 'READING WITH THE EARS'

Individually: one hour

- Your job is to turn a script into a performance.

  The first thing to do with a script is to recreate it as drama in your head. This is tricky. Reading to ourselves, usually we read with our eyes: very quickly. Often we miss important details because the brain fails to register them. What we need to do is to *read with our ears*, listening to the sounds of the words, and letting their full meaning sink in. For example, you will notice some stage directions in this soliloquy. Usually, such things are written in tiny print so they look insignificant.

  In the course of Faustus's final soliloquy, three times a clock strikes. Seeing the stage direction, 'the clock strikes eleven', is not at all like hearing it. To relive that experience, you must pause, allow time for the clock to strike eleven in your imagination: hearing the grim sound the clock makes and feeling the slow, inevitable movement of time. Reading the phrase with the eyes takes less than a second. But *reading it with the ears*, hearing it, as you would in the theatre, might occupy eleven, tense seconds.

  The same is true of the way Faustus talks. There is so much missing from the words when we just read them with our eyes. We need time to latch on to the speaker's tone of voice. To sense how it changes from moment to moment. And we must know the script well before we realize where the silences and the changes of expression come. Because, as we all know from watching great actors, silences and gestures are often more dramatic than the words which surround them.

- As you explore the script, you should also ask yourself these things:
  - which bits should be spoken quickly, which softly?
  - which phrases need to linger to make their impact?
  - which words should be emphasised?

  So when you read-for-feeling, you must be much more aware than usual of the punctuation. That's one of the ways a writer controls the way words are delivered.

- In this version, we have made the punctuation stand out and set out the words to help you read the piece slowly enough for each detail to make maximum impact. So you can learn to *read with your ears*, not just with your eyes.

A still from István Szabó's film *Mephisto* (1981)

*[The clock strikes eleven]*

O, Faustus,

Now hast thou but one bare hour to live,
And then thou must be damned perpetually.

Stand still, you ever moving spheres of heaven,
That time may cease, and midnight never come.
Fair Nature's eye, rise, rise again and make
Perpetual day:

or let this hour be but

A year, a month, a week, a natural day,
That Faustus may repent and save his soul.

**O lente, lente currite, noctis equi! :** 'run slowly, you horses of the night!'

*O lente, lente currite, noctis equi!*

The stars move still, time runs, the clock will strike.
The devil will come, and Faustus must be damned.

O I'll leap up to heaven: who pulls me down?
One drop of blood will save me; O, my Christ! –

**Rend:** split, tear

Rend not my heart for naming of my Christ.
Yet will I call on him: O, spare me Lucifer.

Where is it now? 'Tis gone.
And see a threatening arm, an angry brow.
Mountains and hills, come, come, and fall on me,
And hide me from the heavy wrath of heaven.

No? Then will I headlong run into the earth:
Gape earth! O no, it well not harbour me.

**nativity:** birth

You stars that reigned at my nativity,
Whose influence hath allotted death and hell,
Now draw up Faustus like a foggy mist,
Into the entrails of yon labouring cloud,
That when you vomit forth into the air,
My limbs may issue from your smoky mouths,
So that my soul mount, and ascend to heaven.

*[the watch strikes]*
O, half the hour is past: 'twill all be past anon!

O, if my soul must suffer for my sin
Impose some end to my incessant pain!
Let Faustus live in hell a thousand years,
A hundred thousand, and at last be saved.

No end is limited to damned souls.

**wanting soul:** without a
soul

Why wert thou not a creature wanting soul?
Or why is this immortal that thou hast?

**metempsychosis:** rein-
carnation

O Pythagoras' metempsychosis – were that true,
This soul should fly from me, and I be changed
Into some brutish beast.
All beasts are happy, for when they die,
Their souls are soon dissolved in elements,
But mine must live still to be plagued in hell,

**engendered me:**
produced me

Cursed be the parents that engendered me;

No Faustus, curse thyself, curse Lucifer,
That hath deprived thee of the joys of heaven.

*[The clock strikes midnight]*
It strikes, it strikes! Now body, turn to air,
Or Lucifer will bear thee quick to hell.
O soul be changed into small water drops,
And fall into the ocean, ne'er be found.

*[Thunder, and enter the Devils]*
O mercy heaven, look not so fierce on me;
Adders and serpents, let me breathe awhile!
Ugly hell, gape not! Come not Lucifer!
I'll burn my books! O Mephistophilis!

## THINKING/TALKING POINTS

In groups

Exploring the situation
- Discuss what each of you discovered about Faustus's personality from working on the script. What adjectives do you think best describe him? For example, do you think he comes across as dignified? passionate? calm? resigned? confused? abject? feeble? terrified? ...

- Which moments do you find most disturbing? Most touching?

- How would you describe Faustus's attitude to:
  a) God /Christ
  b) Lucifer/Mephistophilis?

- Who do you think he feels is to blame for his troubles?
  Do you agree with him? Why?

- What feelings do you think an audience would take away from watching this scene?

- Talk about how Marlowe gives us a sense of 'two clocks running' here: the impression of an hour's passing presented in a speech lasting only a few minutes.

Examining the language
- Now look closely at the ways Marlowe dramatises Faustus's state of mind through the way he makes him speak. What questions does he ask? What commands (imperatives) does he use? What do you feel they reveal about his state of mind?

- How does Marlowe convey Faustus's frustration?

- Where is Faustus almost lost for words? Where and why does he repeat things?

- Pick out half a dozen *images* you find particularly powerful. Describe what each one makes you see and feel.

## SECOND ASSIGNMENT

Two hours: choose one

◆ Develop a fully-staged performance of Faustus's final soliloquy. Perform it to the group.

◆ Produce a collage, a storyboard or a picture representing Faustus's final soliloquy: either the whole of it or one particularly powerful image.

◆ 'The final minutes'
Imagine a situation in which somebody today could find him/herself in a situation as terrifying as Faustus does here.

Write a speech suitable for the final scene of the play in which s/he faces up to the fact that time is running out. And why things have turned out as they have. You may write it in prose or try to imitate Marlowe's blank verse.

You will have to decide how far you feel the audience should empathise with the speaker. Try not to 'identify' with your speaker yourself: Faustus is clearly not the person who wrote his speech.

Your creation may be someone who, like Faustus, 'deserves' what's happening to him/her. A criminal, perhaps, or someone who has betrayed people who trusted her/him. But see if you can achieve what Marlowe has perhaps achieved: made the audience feel a sense of pity for someone who has been foolish, careless, perhaps evil ... And a sense of horror at what's about to happen ...

## FOR ADVANCED STUDY: COMPARING TEXTS

Explore the way Shakespeare dramatises the isolation and torment experienced by Lady Macbeth in Act 5 Scene 1of *Macbeth*.

By quoting from and comparing both scenes carefully, describe some of the ways you feel Shakespeare's art is similar to/different from Marlowe's.

# Shakespeare | from *ROMEO AND JULIET*

## THINKING/TALKING POINTS

- Without knowing a great deal about the play they come from or the situations in which the characters find themselves, what is it possible to discover about a speaker's situation from a single soliloquy?

- In the previous unit, Faustus's soliloquy took place in his room at night as he waited, terrified, for the arrival of Mephistophilis.

  Here again, we have a night-time scene. But, in this scene, a young girl awaits the arrival of her new husband.

  Discuss the ways in which the situations of the two characters are similar and different.

- If you were writing Juliet's soliloquy how would you convey her feelings to the audience? How much about her past and present circumstances do you think it would be necessary to reveal to the audience? How would you do that? How would you convey that this is someone to admire or to pity?

**Phoebus:** the sun god

**amorous:** loving

**learn:** teach

> Gallop apace, you fiery-footed steeds,
> Towards Phoebus' lodging; such a waggoner
> As Phaëton would whip you to the west,
> And bring in cloudy night immediately.
> Spread thy close curtain, love-performing Night,
> That runaways' eyes may wink, and Romeo
> Leap to these arms, untalked of and unseen:
> Lovers can see to do their amorous rites
> By their own beauties, or if love be blind,
> It best agrees with night. Come, civil Night,
> Thou sober-suited matron all in black,
> And learn me how to lose a winning match,
> Played for a pair of stainless maidenhoods.
> Hood my unmanned blood, bating in my cheeks,
> With thy black mantle, till strange love grow bold,

Think true love acted simple modesty.
Come, Night, come, Romeo, come, thou day in night,
For thou wilt lie upon the wings of night,
Whiter than new snow upon a raven's back.
Come, gentle Night, come, loving, black-browed Night,
Give me my Romeo, and when I shall die,
Take him and cut him out in little stars,
And he will make the face of heaven so fine
That all the world will be in love with night,
And pay no worship to the garish sun.
0, I have bought the mansion of a love,
But not possessed it, and though I am sold,
Not yet enjoyed. So tedious is this day
As is the night before some festival
To an impatient child that hath new robes
And may not wear them. 0, here comes my Nurse ...

## THINKING/TALKING POINTS

- When you have read or listened to Juliet's soliloquy a few times, discuss your impressions of Juliet's mood, her personality and her situation.

- Pick out six details from the soliloquy which you think are interesting/ beautiful/unexpected. Describe how each one makes you feel.

- Talk about the ways Shakespeare's language conveys a sense of Juliet as:
    a) young
    b) excited
    c) honest
    d) bold.

- Pick out any details which remind you of Faustus's soliloquy in the previous unit. Talk about the ways in which the two soliloquies are similar and different.

## ASSIGNMENT

Choose one: two hours

◆ Prepare a performance of Juliet's soliloquy. Present it to the rest of the group and talk about why you performed it the way you did.

◆ Write an essay comparing Juliet's and Faustus's soliloquies and the ways Shakespeare and Marlowe work on the audiences' feelings in so many different ways during these two short night pieces. Quote a dozen or so details from each soliloquy and talk about how the language works on the audiences' imaginations, thoughts and feelings to generate such different moods in the theatre.

You may want to talk about the images that Faustus and Juliet use, their different tones of voice, the rhythm and tempo of each soliloquy, and the way you imagine these two scenes being presented on stage.

◆ Write a modern version of Juliet's soliloquy. A young girl or boy explores her/his feelings about making love for the first time. The mood may be very different from Juliet's.

You may write it in prose, or see if you can use a modernised version of Shakespeare's blank verse.

### PREPARING A PERFORMANCE

In small groups:
two hours

Characters we meet in plays reveal practically everything about themselves from the way they speak to other people. Usually there is no narrator and we see characters only in the company of someone else. So what we learn about them is limited to some extent by how honest they are. Here are two of Shakespeare's most fascinating characters, Othello and Sir John Falstaff.

Experiment with different ways of performing these extracts and then present them to the rest of the class.

## From *Othello*

Othello is a famous black warrior who serves the Venetian state. He has just married the daughter of one of the Venetian Senators without her father's permission. He is accused publicly of having 'bewitched' her. Here he defends himself against the charge:

> Her father lov'd me, oft invited me,
> Still question'd me the story of my life,
> From year to year; the battles, sieges, fortunes,
> That I have pass'd:
> I ran it through, even from my boyish days,
> To the very moment that he bade me tell it,
> Wherein I spake of most disastrous chances,
> Of moving accidents by flood and field;
> Of hair-breadth scapes i'th' imminent deadly breach;
> Of being taken by the insolent foe;
> And sold to slavery, of my redemption thence,
> And with it all my travel's history;
> Wherein of antres vast, and deserts idle,
> Rough quarries, rocks and hills, whose heads touch heaven,
> It was my hint to speak, such was my process:
> And of the Cannibals,.that each other eat;
> The Anthropophagi, and men whose heads
> Do grow beneath their shoulders: this to hear

Would Desdemona seriously incline;
But still the house-affairs would draw her thence,
And ever as she could with haste dispatch,
She'ld come again, and with a greedy ear
Devour up my discourse; which I observing,
Took once a pliant hour, and found good means
To draw from her a prayer of earnest heart,
That I would all my pilgrimage dilate,
Whereof by parcel she had something heard,
But not intentively. I did consent,
And often did beguile her of her tears,
When I did speak of some distressed stroke
That my youth suffer'd: my story being done,
She gave me for my pains a world of sighs;
She swore i'faith 'twas strange, 'twas passing strange;
'Twas pitiful, 'twas wondrous pitiful;
She wish'd she had not heard it, yet she wish'd
That heaven had made her such a man: she thank'd me,
And bade me, if I had a friend that lov'd her,
I should but teach him how to tell my story,
And that would woo her. Upon this hint I spake:
She lov'd me for the dangers I had pass'd,
And I lov'd her that she did pity them.
This only is the witchcraft I have us'd:
Here comes the lady, let her witness it.

# From *Henry IV Part Two*

Sir John Falstaff is a very large man. Like Othello, he too has a great reputation. Recently he claimed to have killed the mighty rebel Percy at the Battle of Shrewsbury. However, the audience saw that Percy had already been killed by the Prince of Wales, Falstaff's lifelong companion. The court disapproves of their friendship and of their outrageous behaviour together – which includes highway robbery.

*Enter SIR JOHN FALSTAFF alone, followed by his PAGE bearing his sword and buckler.*

FALSTAFF    Sirrah, you giant, what says the doctor to my water?
PAGE   He said, sir, the water itself was a good healthy water; but, for the party that owed it, he might have more diseases than he knew for.
FALSTAFF    Men of all sorts take a pride to gird at me. The brain of this

foolish-compounded clay, man, is not able to invent anything that intends to laughter more than I invent, or is invented on me; I am not only witty in myself, but the cause that wit is in other men. I do here walk before thee like a sow that hath overwhelmed all her litter but one. If the Prince put thee into my service for any other reason than to set me off, why then I have no judgment. Thou whoreson mandrake, thou art fitter to be worn in my cap than to wait at my heels. I was never manned with an agate till now, but I will inset you, neither in gold nor silver, but in vile apparel, and send you back again to your master for a jewel, – the juvenal the Prince your master, whose chin is not yet fledge. I will sooner have a beard grow in the palm of my hand than he shall get one off his cheek; and yet he will not stick to say his face is a face-royal. God may finish it when He will, 'tis not a hair amiss yet. He may keep it still at a face-royal, for a barber shall never earn sixpence out of it. And yet he'll be crowing as if he had writ man ever since his father was a bachelor. He may keep his own grace, but he's almost out of mine, I can assure him. What said Master Dommelton about the satin for my short cloak and my slops?

PAGE  He said, sir, you should procure him better assurance than Bardolph: he would not take his bond and yours, he liked not the security.

FALSTAFF   Let him be damned like the glutton! Pray God his tongue be hotter! A whoreson Achitophel! A rascally yea-forsooth knave, to bear a gentleman in hand, and then stand upon security! The whoreson smooth-pates do now wear nothing but high shoes and bunches of keys at their girdles; and if a man is through with them in honest taking up, then they must stand upon security. I had as lief they would put ratsbane in my mouth as offer to stop it with security. I looked a should have sent me two and twenty yards of satin, as I am a true knight, and he sends me security! Well, he may sleep in security, for he hath the horn of abundance, and the lightness of his wife shines through it; and yet cannot he see, though he have his own lanthorn to light him. Where's Bardolph?

PAGE   He's gone into Smithfield to buy your worship a horse.

FALSTAFF   I bought him in Paul's, and he'll buy me a horse in Smithfield. And I could get me but a wife in the stews, I were manned, horsed, and wived.

*Enter LORD CHIEF JUSTICE and SERVANT.*

PAGE   Sir, here comes the nobleman that committed the Prince for striking him about Bardolph.

FALSTAFF    Wait close, I will not see him.

CHIEF JUSTICE    What's he that goes there?

SERVANT    Falstaff, and't please your lordship.

CHIEF JUSTICE    He that was in question for the robbery?

SERVANT    He, my lord: but he hath since done good service at Shrewsbury, and, as I hear, is now going with some charge to the Lord John of Lancaster.

CHIEF JUSTICE    What, to York? Call him back again.

SERVANT    Sir John Falstaff!

FALSTAFF    Boy, tell him I am deaf.

PAGE    You must speak louder, my master is deaf.

CHIEF JUSTICE    I am sure he is, to the hearing of anything good. Go pluck him by the elbow, I must speak with him.

SERVANT    Sir John!

FALSTAFF    What! A young knave, and begging! Is there not wars? Is there not employment? Doth not the King lack subjects? Do not the rebels need soldiers? Though it be a shame to be on any side but one, it is worse shame to beg than to be on the worst side, were it worse than the name of rebellion can tell how to make it.

SERVANT    You mistake me, sir.

FALSTAFF    Why, sir, did I say you were an honest man? Setting my knighthood and my soldiership aside, I had lied in my throat if I had said so.

SERVANT    I pray you, sir, then set your knighthood and your soldiership aside, and give me leave to tell you lie in your throat if you say I am any other than an honest man.

FALSTAFF    I give thee leave to tell me so? I lay aside that which grows to me? If thou get'st any leave of me, hang me. If thou tak'st leave, thou wert better be hanged. You hunt counter. Hence! Avaunt!

SERVANT    Sir, my lord would speak with you.

CHIEF JUSTICE    Sir John Falstaff, a word with you.

FALSTAFF    My good lord! God give your lordship good time of day. I am glad to see your lordship abroad, I heard say your lordship was sick. I hope your lordship goes abroad by advice; your lordship, though not clean past your youth, have yet some smack of age in you, some relish of the saltness of time; and I most humbly beseech your lordship to have a reverend care of your health.

CHIEF JUSTICE    Sir John, I sent for you before your expedition to Shrewsbury.

FALSTAFF    And't please your lordship, I hear his Majesty is returned with some discomfort from Wales.

CHIEF JUSTICE    I talk not of his Majesty. You would not come when I sent for you.

FALSTAFF   And I hear, moreover, his Highness is fallen into this same whoreson apoplexy.

CHIEF JUSTICE   Well, God mend him! I pray you, let me speak with you.

FALSTAFF   This apoplexy, as I take it, is a kind of lethargy, and't please your lordship, a kind of sleeping in the blood, a whoreson tingling.

CHIEF JUSTICE   What tell you me of it? Be it as it is.

FALSTAFF   It hath it original from much grief, from study, and perturbation of the brain; I have read the cause of his effects in Galen, it is a kind of deafness.

CHIEF JUSTICE   I think you are fallen into the disease, for you hear not what I say to you.

FALSTAFF   Very well, my lord, very well. Rather, and't please you, it is the disease of not listening, the malady of not marking, that I am troubled withal.

CHIEF JUSTICE   To punish you by the heels would amend the attention of your ears, and I care not if I do become your physician.

FALSTAFF   I am as poor as Job, my lord, but not so patient. Your lordship may minister the potion of imprisonment to me in respect of poverty; but how I should be your patient to follow your prescriptions, the wise may make some dram of a scruple, or indeed a scruple itself.

CHIEF JUSTICE   I sent for you, when there were matters against you for your life, to come speak with me.

FALSTAFF   As I was then advised by my learned counsel in the laws of this land-service, I did not come.

CHIEF JUSTICE   Well, the truth is, Sir John, you live in great infamy.

FALSTAFF   He that buckles himself in my belt cannot live in less.

CHIEF JUSTICE   Your means are very slender, and your waste is great.

FALSTAFF   I would it were otherwise, I would my means were greater and my waist slenderer.

CHIEF JUSTICE   You have misled the youthful Prince.

FALSTAFF   The young Prince hath misled me. I am the fellow with the great belly, and he my dog.

CHIEF JUSTICE   Well, I am loath to gall a new-healed wound. Your day's service at Shrewsbury hath a little gilded over your night's exploit on Gad's Hill. You may thank th' unquiet time for your quiet o'er-posting that action.

FALSTAFF   My lord! –

CHIEF JUSTICE   But since all is well, keep it so: wake not a sleeping wolf.

FALSTAFF   To wake a wolf is as bad as smell a fox.

CHIEF JUSTICE   What! You are as a candle, the better part burnt out.

FALSTAFF   A wassail candle, my lord, all tallow – if I did say of wax, my growth would approve the truth.

CHIEF JUSTICE    There is not a white hair in your face but should have his effect of gravity.

FALSTAFF    His effect of gravy, gravy, gravy.

CHIEF JUSTICE    You follow the young Prince up and down, like his ill angel.

FALSTAFF    Not so, my lord, your ill angel is light, but I hope he that looks upon me will take me without weighing. And yet in some respects, I grant, I cannot go. I cannot tell – virtue is of so little regard in these costermongers' times that true valour is turned bearherd; pregnancy is made a tapster, and his quick wit wasted in giving reckonings; all the other gifts appertinent to man, as the malice of this age shapes them, are not worth a gooseberry. You that are old consider not the capacities of us that are young; you do measure the heat of our livers with the bitterness of your galls; and we that are in the vaward of our youth, I must confess, are wags too.

CHIEF JUSTICE    Do you set down your name in the scroll of youth, that are written down old with all the characters of age? Have you not a moist eye, a dry hand, a yellow cheek, a white beard, a decreasing leg, an increasing belly? Is not your voice broken, your wind short, your chin double, your wit single, and every part about you blasted with antiquity? And will you yet call yourself young? Fie, fie, fie, Sir John!

FALSTAFF    My lord, I was born about three of the clock in the afternoon, with a white head, and something a round belly. For my voice, I have lost it with hallooing, and singing of anthems. To approve my youth further, I will not; the truth is, I am only old in judgment and understanding; and he that will caper with me for a thousand marks, let him lend me the money, and have at him! For the box of the ear that the Prince gave you, he gave it like a rude prince, and you took it like a sensible lord. I have checked him for it, and the young lion repents – [*Aside*] marry, not in ashes and sackcloth, but in new silk and old sack.

CHIEF JUSTICE    Well, God send the Prince a better companion!

FALSTAFF    God send the companion a better prince! I cannot rid my hands of him.

CHIEF JUSTICE    Well, the King hath severed you and Prince Harry: I hear you are going with Lord John of Lancaster, against the Archbishop and the Earl of Northumberland.

FALSTAFF    Yea, I thank your pretty sweet wit for it. But look you pray, all you that kiss my lady Peace at home, that our armies join not in a hot day; for, by the Lord, I take but two shirts out with me, and I mean not to sweat extraordinarily. If it be a hot day, and I brandish anything but a bottle, I would I might never spit white again. There is not a dangerous action can peep out his head but I am thrust upon it. Well, I cannot last ever; but it was always yet the trick of our English nation, if they have a good thing, to make it too common. If ye will needs say I am an old man, you should give me rest. I would to God my name were not so terrible to the enemy as it is – I were better to be eaten to death with a rust than to be scoured to nothing with perpetual motion.

CHIEF JUSTICE  Well, be honest, be honest, and God bless your expedition!

FALSTAFF  Will your lordship lend me a thousand pound to furnish me forth?

CHIEF JUSTICE  Not a penny, not a penny; you are too impatient to bear crosses. Fare you well: commend me to my cousin Westmoreland.

*Exeunt CHIEF JUSTICE and SERVANT.*

FALSTAFF  If I do, fillip me with a three-man beetle. A man can no more separate age and covetousness than a can part young limbs and lechery: but the gout galls the one, and the pox pinches the other; and so both the degrees prevent my curses. Boy!

PAGE  Sir?

FALSTAFF  What money is in my purse?

PAGE  Seven groats and two pence.

FALSTAFF  I can get no remedy against this consumption of the purse; borrowing only lingers and lingers it out, but the disease is incurable. Go bear this letter to my Lord of Lancaster; this to the Prince; this to the Earl of Westmoreland; – and this to old mistress Ursula, whom I have weekly sworn to marry since I perceived the first white hair of my chin. About it; you know where to find me. [*Exit PAGE.*]  A pox of this gout! or a gout of this pox! for the one or the other plays the rogue with my great toe. 'Tis no matter if I do halt; I have the wars for my colour, and my pension shall seem the more reasonable. A good wit will make use of anything; I will turn diseases to commodity.

*[Exit]*

## PLENARY

- Discuss what you learned about Falstaff and Othello from your performances.

- How far did you find yourself getting to like these characters as you became familiar with their very different ways of talking?

- Do you think the audience is expected to feel critical of either – or both – of them? Why?

- Look through the extracts again for a few minutes. Pick out some details which you feel bring out each character's a) strengths, and b) weaknesses.

- Discuss what you think worked well in each of your performances and ways in which they could be even better.

- Polish your performances and then make a video of them to put into the library for others to enjoy.

A still from Neil Jordan's film *The Company of Wolves* (1984)

# *Ted Hughes* | THE HOWLING OF WOLVES
# *Angela Carter* | from *THE COMPANY OF WOLVES*

In this unit you will explore two powerful pieces of writing about wolves: the poem 'The Howling of Wolves' by Ted Hughes, and an extract from the novel *The Company of Wolves* by Angela Carter.

## THINKING/TALKING POINTS

*Individually, then in small groups*

- On your own, jot down on a notepad whatever comes into your mind, triggered by the word 'wolves'. Think about:
  - stories you've heard, films you've seen, visits you've made to the zoo
  - shapes, smells, colours, textures and sounds
  - the kind of weather, time of day, seasons
  - the terrain wolves inhabit.

- Then, in your groups, discuss the ideas and images each of you associated with wolves. Explain to the rest of the group how/why the word 'wolves' ignited those particular thoughts.

- Choose someone to act as scribe and arrange on a large sheet of paper the various words and phrases people come up with. Talk about the best way of arranging the words and phrases on the sheet.

- Display your sheet and compare it with those produced by the other groups.

## FIRST ASSIGNMENT: CREATIVE WRITING

*Individually/in small groups*

◆ String together some of the words and images you came up with in the brainstorm. Add to them, then develop them, either as the opening page of a short story or as a poem.

Consider the different demands of the two kinds of writing.

**A short story**
If you are writing the opening page of a short story, think about how you will tell the story:
  - in the first or the third person?

- in the present or the past tense?
- will it describe a place or introduce some of the characters in the story? Or will it do both?
- what kind of mood do you wish to create? What length of sentences, what kind of vocabulary, what sort of imagery will help you to do that?
- what sort of reader is it intended for?

### A poem

If you are writing a poem, think about how you will structure it:
- will the piece have a regular or an irregular shape?
- will each line contain a certain number of syllables or stresses?
- will you use rhyme? If so, why and in what pattern?
- will the poem be written as if spoken by someone involved in the situation, or by someone observing it?
- will the language be like/unlike everyday speech? Why?

When you are satisfied with your piece, give it a suitable title. Make a neat copy. You may wish to work some illustrations into the final presentation.

### PLENARY

Display your finished piece and discuss the similarities and differences in the pieces you've generated.

## The Howling of Wolves

Is without world.

What are they dragging up and out on their long leashes of sound
That dissolve in the mid-air silence?

Then crying of a baby, in this forest of starving silences,
Brings the wolves running.
Tuning of a viola, in this forest delicate as an owl's ear,
Brings the wolves running – brings the steel traps clashing and
    slavering,
The steel furred to keep it from cracking in the cold,

The eyes that never learn how it has come about
That they must live like this,

That they must live

Innocence crept into minerals.

The wind sweeps through and the hunched wolf shivers.
It howls you cannot say whether out of agony or joy.

The earth is under its tongue,
A dead weight of darkness, trying to see through its eyes.
The wolf is living for the earth.
But the wolf is small, it comprehends little.

It goes to and fro, trailing its haunches and whimpering horribly.

It must feed its fur.

The night snows stars and the earth creaks.

## THINKING/TALKING POINTS

- When you have heard or read through the poem three or four times, jot down from memory as many details as you can remember. Talk about the details you recalled: what did they make you feel, see, hear, imagine?

- Imagine a painting inspired by the poem. Describe the picture to each other.

- Look at the way the poem is set out on the page. Discuss why you think the words were set out in this way.

- Choose a complete sentence from the poem and write it out in a different way. Discuss whether the way you have set out the sentence changes the impact it has when you see it, or the way you would read it aloud.

- Reread the poem a couple of times around the class, taking a complete sentence in turn.

# From *The Company of Wolves*

One beast and only one howls in the woods by night.

The wolf is carnivore incarnate and he's as cunning as he is ferocious; once he's had a taste of flesh then nothing else will do.

At night, the eyes of wolves shine like candle flames, yellowish, reddish, but that is because the pupils of their eyes fatten on darkness and catch the light from your lantern to flash it back to you – red for danger; if a wolf's eyes reflect only moonlight, then they gleam a cold and unnatural green, a mineral, a piercing colour. If the benighted traveller spies those luminous, terrible sequins stitched suddenly on the black thickets, then he knows he must run, if fear has not struck him stock-still.

But those eyes are all you will be able to glimpse of the forest assassins as they cluster invisibly round your smell of meat as you go through the wood unwisely late. They will be like shadows, they will be like wraiths, grey members of a congregation of nightmare; hark! his long, wavering howl... an aria of fear made audible.

The wolfsong is the sound of the rending you will suffer, in itself a murdering.

It is winter and cold weather. In this region of mountain and forest, there is now nothing for the wolves to eat. Goats and sheep are locked up in the byre, the deer departed for the remaining pasturage on the southern slopes – wolves grow lean and famished. There is so little flesh on them that you could count the starveling ribs through their pelts, if they gave you time before they pounced. Those slavering jaws; the lolling tongue; the rime of saliva on the grizzled chops – of all the teeming perils of the night and the forest, ghosts, hobgoblins, ogres that grill babies upon gridirons, witches that fatten their captives in cages for cannibal tables, the wolf is the worst for he cannot listen to reason.

## THINKING/TALKING POINTS

- When you have heard/read the piece a couple of times, jot down from memory as many details as you can recall.

- Talk about the details which stuck in your memory. Did you remember particular words or particular ideas or both? Describe what each of those details made you feel, see, hear and imagine.

- Imagine a painting or an animated film inspired by that piece. Describe it to each other.

- Read through the passage a couple of times. What do you notice about the way Angela Carter's prose is written? How is it like/unlike the writing you might find in a textbook about wild animals? Think about the lengths of the sentences, the vocabulary, the imagery. Why do you think Angela Carter decided to write in the present tense?

- What are some of the similarities/differences between the poem and the extract?

Now listen to or read both pieces again.

## SECOND ASSIGNMENT

**Choose one: two hours**

◆ Performance: in pairs/small groups
Choose one of the pieces to work on. Read it through a few times, sharing out the lines between you. Discuss some ways of performing the piece to an audience of twelve-year olds.

Would you present it simply as sound, or use actions and images as well? At what tempo do you think the piece would work best? Where would you raise, where lower your voice? Where would you pause to let certain details sink in?

Either on your own or with others, make a tape/video recording of your performance. You may like to write a commentary on how you prepared your presentation and why you did it in the way you did.

◆ Critical essay: 'Ted Hughes and Angela Carter writing about wolves: similarities and differences'
After reading through the notes you have made, look again at the way the two pieces are presented on the page. One is set out as a poem, the other as prose. Study both pieces carefully, reading them through aloud a few times. Jot down any new ideas which come to you as you compare the two pieces of work.

Do you think the way they are set out makes an important difference to the experience of a) hearing, b) reading them? Why?

Write an essay comparing the two pieces. Quote and comment in some detail upon six or so moments in each piece. Talk about the impact the two pieces made on you. Did you feel they were very similar or quite different? Now you know them both well, do you find one more disturbing/powerful/confusing than the other? Explain why. What sort of audience do you think each piece was intended for? You might like to consider whether either or both of the pieces were intended to be humorous.

## EXTENSION ASSIGNMENT: PASTICHE OR PARODY

**Choose one**

Read through both pieces again a few times, aloud if possible. Then choose the one you like most, or the one which you think has any particular weaknesses in it, on which to write a pastiche or a parody. Write *either* the second part of the poem *or* the next few paragraphs of the story.

◆ Pastiche

In your pastiche, try to imitate the layout and the style of the original as carefully as you can. Be particularly aware of the tone of voice the original piece suggests to you. Use a similar layout, similar vocabulary and similar ideas.

Write a commentary, describing which features of the original you were trying to copy and how you went about doing so. Illustrate your points with quotations from the original piece and from your extension.

◆ Parody

If you feel the piece is badly written in some way, use your parody to exaggerate the weaknesses you perceive.

Write a commentary, using quotations from the original and from your parody to explain what stylistic features you were mocking and why. Describe how you went about your task.

*Shakespeare* | from *HENRY V*

*Hopkins* | from *THE WRECK OF THE DEUTSCHLAND*

*Byron* | *THE DESTRUCTION OF SENNACHERIB*

One of the most powerful tools writers use is imagery.
An image is a picture-in-words. As you close your eyes and surrender to the poem or prose piece, words transform into powerful pictures in your mind.

Images in poems are different from the images in films and on television because what each of us 'sees' in our minds depends upon who we are. It depends upon everything already in our heads: all our experiences, our memories, the ways we think: in other words our 'imagination'. No two people have the same imaginary picture in their heads of Oliver Twist or the Queen of the Night or Count Dracula.

Talk about how each of you imagines these characters.

## From *Henry V*

Shakespeare was a poet who wrote mainly for the stage. The theatre in which his plays were performed had none of the gizmos which someone making a film today uses to make the audience believe what they're watching is 'real'. Shakespeare relied on the audience's imagination to 'piece out' what happened on the bare boards.

His play *Henry V* begins with an apology. It is a brilliant demonstration of how poetry works. Shakespeare tells us his play relies upon audience participation. He can't possibly present the Battle of Agincourt realistically. We can't just sit there and watch. We must 'piece out' the shortcomings of the theatre with our imaginations.

> ... pardon, gentles all,
> The flat unraised spirits, that hath dared,
> On this unworthy scaffold, to bring forth
> So great an object.
>                         Can this cockpit hold

The vasty fields of France?

                                    Or may we cram

**casques:** cannon

Within this wooden nought the very casques
That did affright the air at Agincourt?

Oh, pardon: ...
And let us,
On your imaginary forces work.

                    Suppose within the girdle of these walls
Are now confined two mighty monarchies,
Whose high upreared and abutting fronts
The perilous narrow ocean parts asunder.

Piece out our imperfections with your thoughts.

Into a thousand parts divide one man,

**puissance:** strength;
armies

And make imaginary puissance.

Think when we talk of horses that you see them
Printing their proud hooves i'th' receiving earth ...

## THINKING/TALKING POINTS

* Close your eyes and listen while someone reads out those last two lines
  again.

  *Think* when we talk of horses *that you see them*
  Printing their proud hooves i'th' receiving earth ...

  What do you hear, exactly? What does it make you see?

* Discuss how the sounds of the words

  Printing their proud hooves i'th' receiving earth ...

help to generate the illusion that we experience what's being described.
It's not simply that we see the proud horses' hooves leaving their mark in
the soft ground. We hear them doing it, too. The rhythm of the line, the
stresses which fall, imitate the thud of horses' hooves on the turf.

What we have is a super-image. A moving picture with sound —
Shakespeare was making films long before the cinema was invented.

- Shakespeare doesn't use imagery simply to make up for the lack of elaborate props, scenery and special effects when he's writing for the stage. An image is worth a hundred image-less words. Like most poets, Shakespeare regularly translates abstract things such as fear, jealousy, grief, anger and guilt into powerful pictures.

  For example, when Macbeth feels tortured to the point of insanity with the guilt he feels for slaughtering the King, he says to his partner:

  Full of scorpions is my mind, dear wife

  Talk about all the reasons why that image is so disturbing.

- Have a go at representing Macbeth's words as a drawing.


## STORYBOARDING 1

One hour

Here are some other examples of images taken from a dozen Shakespeare plays.

In each case, think about how you could represent the image as a poster or as a frame in an animated version of the play. Some snippets could be presented 'realistically'. Others work only in the realms of the imagination. You would have to use an appropriately surreal style of drawing.

In some cases you'll find there are enough images for several frames.

> when he walks, he moves like an engine, and the ground shrinks before his treading ...

> The friends thou hast, and their adoption tried,
> Grapple them to thy soul with hoops of steel ...

> Aye, but to die and go we know not where;
> To lie in cold obstruction, and to rot;
> This sensible and warm motion to become
> A kneaded clod; and the delighted spirit
> To bathe in fiery floods, or to reside
> In thrilling regions of thick-ribbed ice;
> To be imprisoned in the viewless winds
> And blown with restless violence round about
> The pendent world ...

Petruchio is coming, in a new hat and an old jerkin; a pair of old breeches thrice turned; a pair of boots that have been candle-cases, one buckled, another lac'd; an old rusty sword taken out of the town-armoury, with a broken hilt, and chapless ...

To the dread rattling thunder
Have I given fire, and rifted Jove's stout oak
With his own bolt; the strong-based promontory
Have I made shake; and by the spurs plucked up
The pine and cedar. Graves at my command
Have waked their sleepers, oped and let them forth ...

   Get thee glass eyes;
And, like a scurvy politician, seem
To see the things thou dost not

a man made after supper of a cheese-paring

   the toad, ugly and venomous,
Wears yet a precious jewel in his head

there is a devil haunts thee in the likeness of an old fat man; a tun of man is thy companion. Why dost thou converse with that trunk of humours, that bolting-hutch of beastliness, that swollen parcel of dropsies, that huge bombard of sack, that stuffed cloakbag of guts, that roasted Manningtree ox with the pudding in his belly ...?

   the whining school-boy, with his satchel
And shining morning face, creeping like snail
Unwillingly to school

Grim-visaged war hath smoothed his wrinkled front,
And now, instead of mounting barbed steeds
To fright the souls of fearful adversaries,
He capers nimbly in a lady's chamber
To the lascivious pleasing of a lute

See, how she leans her cheek upon her hand

# From *The Wreck of the Deutschland*

Before we look at the work of another poet, think about how you might draw a picture of Death. Death bragging about his strength – and about all the horrible ways he can end people's lives.

Here are some lines from a poem written about a hundred and twenty years ago. Read or listen to these lines four times.

> 'Some find me a sword; some
> The flange and the rail; flame,
> Fang, or flood' goes Death on drum,
> And storms bugle his fame.

## STORYBOARDING 2

**Twenty minutes**

You have been asked to make a storyboard for these four lines. It will be used in an animated version of the poem. The whole piece is about a terrible shipwreck off the east coast of England which happened in a treacherous blizzard in 1875. In the four lines you are storyboarding, Death is bragging about his many ways of destroying us.

Compare and discuss your storyboards.

Here's the complete stanza from which those four lines came. Now try storyboarding the second half.

> 'Some find me a sword; some
> The flange and the rail; flame,
> Fang, or flood' goes Death on drum,
> And storms bugle his fame.
> But we dream we are rooted in earth – Dust!
> Flesh falls within sight of us, we, though our flower the same,
> Wave with the meadow, forget that there must
> The sour scythe cringe, and the blear share come.

On page 158, you will find a storyboard of this stanza done by a Year Twelve student, Polina Bakhnova. Compare it with the ones you produced.

## STORYBOARDING 3

**In small groups: two hours**

You're now going to attempt to storyboard an entire poem. It's one which has been popular ever since it was written: few anthologies of English poetry leave it out. Like the Hopkins extract, it describes a terrible event. But the words are so powerful, so evocative, so musical, that it's difficult not to be excited by them.

Begin by preparing a reading. Perform the poem a few times until you have most of the words by heart.

Discuss how your team might go about storyboarding the whole poem. Decide who will do what and by what deadlines. Present your finished piece to the rest of the class.

## *The Destruction of Sennacherib*

The Assyrian came down like the wolf on the fold,
And his cohorts were gleaming in purple and gold;
And the sheen of their spears was like stars on the sea,
When the blue wave rolls nightly on deep Galilee.

Like the leaves of the forest when Summer is green,
That host with their banners at sunset were seen:
Like the leaves of the forest when Autumn hath blown,
That host on the morrow lay withered and strown.

For the Angel of Death spread his wings on the blast,
And breathed in the face of the foe as he passed;
And the eyes of the sleepers waxed deadly and chill,
And their hearts but once heaved – and for ever grew still!

And there lay the steed with his nostril all wide,
But through it there rolled not the breath of his pride;
And the foam of his gasping lay white on the turf,
And cold as the spray of the rock-beating surf.

And there lay the rider distorted and pale,
With the dew on his brow, and the rust on his mail:
And the tents were all silent – the banners alone –
The lances unlifted – the trumpet unblown.

And the widows of Ashur are loud in their wail,
And the idols are broke in the temple of Baal;
And the might of the Gentile, unsmote by the sword,
Hath melted like snow in the glance of the Lord!

Seaham, 17th February 1815

## PRELIMINARY ASSIGNMENT

15 minutes

◆ Write the word 'City' at the top of a sheet of paper.

Close your eyes. Imagine yourself alone in a large city late at night. What do you see and hear? What can you smell, taste and touch?

Perhaps you remember some night you found yourself in an unfamiliar city. What impressions, sensations, feelings do you recall?

Now, quickly jot down as many words and phrases as you can to describe the sights, sounds and smells of the place you remember, and to convey your thoughts and feelings about being in that city at night. It might look something like this:

Energy pulsing
Grubby, exciting
Neons flashing
Bright, loud as a fairground
Sickly smells of strange food
Silent, deserted like a tomb
Like a maze
Shop windows shuttered
So many long, cold, hard streets
Something/Someone huddled up in
a doorway – Dead or Alive?
Strangers' eyes
Classy mannequins staring out hard-eyed
Faceless, fast black taxis
Oily puddles.     Slippery alleyways
Where to find the bus stop? The station?
Two shiny coins in the gutter
Black bin bags spilling

Now choose just a dozen words or phrases from your list and put them into some sort of order: as a list, as a poem, as a short piece of prose. Share your writing with the others.

Here is a poem written about two hundred years ago. Brought up far away from the city, in the wild and rugged Lake District and loving its landscape of rocks, lakes, mountains and waterfalls, this writer came to London as a stranger.

Before you read it, talk about what you think that visitor to London might have felt as he walked across Westminster Bridge very early one morning.

## Composed upon Westminster Bridge

Sept. 3, 1802

Earth has not any thing to show more fair:
    Dull would he be of soul who could pass by
    A sight so touching in its majesty:
This City now doth like a garment wear
The beauty of the morning; silent, bare,
    Ships, towers, domes, theatres, and temples lie
    Open unto the fields, and to the sky;
All bright and glittering in the smokeless air.
Never did sun more beautifully steep
    In his first splendor valley, rock or hill;
Ne'er saw I, never felt, a calm so deep!
    The river glideth at his own sweet will:
Dear God! the very houses seem asleep;
    And all that mighty heart is lying still!

*William Wordsworth*

### THINKING/TALKING POINTS

**In groups**

- Describe your first impressions of a) the speaker's mood, and b) the city the speaker sees.

- Reread or listen to the poem again a couple of times. From memory, jot down three or four words or phrases which you feel set the poem's mood. Read out your choices to each other. Talk about why you think you remembered those particular words or phrases. What did each of them make you feel, imagine, visualise?

- Try sketching something the poem described.

- Now read the poem around the group a couple of times, taking a sentence in turn. How would you describe a) the tone, and b) the tempo of this poem? Would you choose any of these words to describe them?

| | | | |
|---|---|---|---|
| hurried | angry | reflective | easy-going |
| steady | impatient | tense | stately |
| happy | edgy | ecstatic | tranquil |
| plodding | rapt | enthralled | tender |

- When you wrote your own piece about a city at the beginning of the unit, how was it similar to/different from this one? What were the key words/phrases in your piece? What words best describe its tone and tempo?

## SECOND ASSIGNMENT

One hour

◆ Imagine yourself walking the streets of a city late at night or early in the morning. You are alone. Picture in your mind the sights; hear in your head the sounds which tell you this is the big city you're in, not the countryside.

Now concentrate on the flavours, the smells and tastes of a particular city, the movement/stillness. How are the air you breathe and the atmosphere you feel very different in such a place at such a time from what you'd experience anywhere else?

Imagine taking five snapshots to capture the character of the place you are in. What will you photograph? How would someone seeing those snapshots know it was a city today, not one in 1802? If you taped five characteristic city noises, what would they be?

Go through all your jottings and develop your piece. Decide what mood you wish to share with your readers. Decide what images, sounds, tempo and tone best fit your feelings. Choose half a dozen strong pictures/sensations around which to construct your piece.

You may like to try to write a poem similar in shape to Wordsworth's. Look at his poem again. See if you can work out how it is put together. How long is it? How many syllables are there in each line? Where do the rhymes come – and the pauses?

You may prefer to use a different poetic form, or to write in prose. Your piece should be no more than 110 words long.

Doré: 'A City Thoroughfare'

# City poems

## THINKING/TALKING POINTS

- When did Wordsworth write his sonnet describing the view from Westminster Bridge?

- Here are five more poems about the city and what it's like living there. They were written in 1865, 1899, 1900, 1981 and 1993. However, they are not printed in the order in which they were written. As you work on your poem, discuss which of those dates you feel best fits it, and why.

## PREPARING A PERFORMANCE

In groups: thirty minutes

- Divide into five groups with each group working on a single poem. Begin by reading the poem silently to yourselves a few times. Then read the poem aloud around the group, each taking a whole sentence in turn. Don't worry about the details you don't fully understand. Keep the poem moving.

- Talk about the mood you feel your poem conveys, and how best to bring that out in your presentation. Discuss any details that people find puzzling.

- Read the poem around the group again a few times. Don't rush. Read your sentence so that someone hearing it for the first time will pick up not just the sense but the mood of the lines you're speaking.

- If there is time, experiment with different ways of presenting your poem. You could read some lines as a whole group, some lines or certain key words with a single voice. You could have some people reading, some people miming to the poem, like a silent film with a voice-over. You could turn your piece into a song, into a chant, or into a series of frozen tableaux. Maybe you'd like to represent the poem as a storyboard, with someone reading the text as each frame is displayed.

This poem is like a still-life painting.

## In a London Drawing Room

The sky is cloudy, yellowed by the smoke.
For view there are the houses opposite
Cutting the sky with one long line of wall
Like solid fog: far as the eye can stretch
Monotony of surface and of form
Without a break to hang a guess upon.

No bird can make a shadow as it flies,
For all is shadow, as in ways o'erhung
By thickest canvass, where the golden rays
Are clothed in hemp. No figure lingering
Pauses to feed the hunger of the eye
Or rest a little on the lap of life.

All hurry on and look upon the ground,
Or glance unmarking at the passers by.
The wheels are hurrying too, cabs, carriages
All closed, in multiplied identity.
The world seems one huge prison-house and court
Where men are punished at the slightest cost,
With lowest rate of colour, warmth and joy.

In this poem, we glimpse one city-dweller's private territory.

## Room

One chair to sit in,
a greasy dusk wrong side of the tracks,
and watch the lodgers' lights come on in the other rooms.

No curtains yet. A cool lightbulb
waiting for a moth. Hard silence.
The roofs of terraced houses stretch from here to how many
months.

Room. One second-hand bed
to remind of a death, somewhen. Room.
Then clouds the colour of smokers' lungs. Then what.

In a cold black window, a face
takes off its glasses and stares out again.
Night now; the giftless moon and a cat pissing on a wall. £90pw.

This speaker celebrates moving from the countryside to the city.

# London

Farewell, sweetest country; out of my heart, you roses,
Wayside roses, nodding, the slow traveller to keep.
Too long have I drowsed alone in the meadows deep,
Too long alone endured the silence Nature espouses.
Oh, the rush, the rapture of life! throngs, lights, houses,
This is London. I wake as a sentinel from sleep.

**sentinel:** sentry on duty

Stunned with the fresh thunder, the harsh delightful noises,
I move entranced on the thronging pavement. How sweet,
To eyes sated with green, the dusty brick-walled street!
And the lone spirit, of self so weary, how it rejoices
To be lost in others, bathed in the tones of human voices,
And feel hurried along the happy tread of feet.

**sated:** fed up

And a sense of vast sympathy my heart almost crazes,
The warmth of kindred hearts in thousands beating with mine.
Each fresh face, each figure, my spirit drinks like wine, –
Thousands endlessly passing. Violets, daisies,
What is your charm to the passionate charm of faces,
This ravishing reality, this earthliness divine?

O murmur of men more sweet than all the wood's caresses,
How sweet only to be an unknown leaf that sings
In the forest of life! Cease, Nature, thy whisperings.
Can I talk with leaves, or fall in love with breezes?
Beautiful boughs, your shade not a human pang appeases.
This is London. I lie, and twine in the roots of things.

**appeases:** makes better

This speaker does some rhythmical grumbling.

# View from the Window

Mathematical shapes creep in at the door,
Geometric squares stare up from the floor.
The ceiling is white – it used to be blue –
And the dope of this world is benzene-based glue.

An architect lives in a house on the green,
The windows are bay and the paintwork is clean,
But what he designed for my family
Was a garden of concrete with breeze-block for sky.

The stairways are signed by unknown hands,
The balconies filled with fields of tin-cans.
The view from the window's the view from the door,
And the view from the roof is the view from the floor.

Aeons ago a man thought he would try
To design a prison to scratch the sky;
The walls would be built of blood, sweat and toil
While the country around he aimed to despoil.

He employed the armies of death and decay,
Architects' strategies were put on display,
Dividers and callipers goose-stepped with pride
But the cartridge was paper, and the rules only slide.

Towering siege-weapons dismembered the view
As a mass of black spears serrated the blue.
Finally the tower of doom was complete
And remaining problems were solved by deceit.

He ushered us in, and was then called away;
Now the children of despair come here to play.

Here we are made to see the city as if it were a person.

# London

See what a mass of gems the city wears
Upon her broad live bosom! row on row
Rubies and emeralds and amethysts glow.
See! that huge circle, like a necklace, stares
With thousands of bold eyes to heaven, and dares
The golden stars to dim the lamps below,
And in the mirror of the mire I know
The moon has left her image unawares.
That's the great town at night: I see her breasts;
Pricked out with lamps they stand like huge black towers,
I think they move! I hear her panting breath.
And that's her head where the tiara rests.
And in her brain, through lanes as dark as death,
Men creep like thoughts ...
The lamps are like pale flowers.

## PLENARY

One hour

- When you've heard each of the poems performed a couple of times, discuss what you find interesting/effective/distinctive a) about each of the poems and b) about the way the group presented it.

- How was each poem about the city similar to/different from Wordsworth's? In what ways?

- Which poems do you think revealed most about the speakers? How did they do that?

- Which lines came closest to matching your own thoughts about city life when you made your chart? In what ways?

- Now listen again to each poem while somebody else reads them once more. Here are some more things you may like to discuss about each poem: the tone and the style, its images, the vocabulary it uses, the shape, the way the poet uses rhythm and rhyme.

## THIRD ASSIGNMENT

Choose one: one hour

◆ Taking 'Room' or one of the London poems as a starting point, imagine you are a student newly-arrived in an unfamiliar city from a very different environment. Write a letter home, describing your first impressions of your new home.

Write in the first person, as if you're the student.
Describe your experiences as you found your way around the unfamiliar city, searched for and finally found somewhere to live, and your feelings as you think about what life in your new surroundings will be like.

◆ Write a study of two or three poems from this unit. How are they similar? How are they different? You may like to compare them with Wordsworth's sonnet too. Remember to structure your essay around a dozen or so brief quotations. Talk about what you find striking about the language of the quotations you choose.

## RESEARCH ASSIGNMENT

Two hours: choose one

◆ The poets whose work appears in this unit are: Carol Ann Duffy, David Green, George Eliot, Alfred Douglas and Manmohan Ghose. See if by searching in the library you can discover who wrote which poem and when.

What can you find out about the poets' lives and the world in which they worked? Do you think this helps to explain some of the feelings explored in their poems?

Prepare a summary of your findings to give to the class.

◆ Using this unit as a model, devise a study pack called *Experiences of the Countryside*. It should be suitable for use by Year Nine students.

Start your work in the library, searching out as many poems which deal with country life as you can. You may find anthologies/CD ROMs which group poems by theme or topic. From all the poems you discover, choose seven or eight contrasting ones around which to structure your study pack.

Begin your unit by encouraging people to explore their own feelings, memories and expectations of country life. Then think of the best ways to explore the handful of poems you've selected to show the different ways people see country life, some stressing the pluses, others presenting such life as grim.

Your study pack will work best if you make a carefully-prepared sound recording of the poems for your students to listen to.

Here are some thought-stirring poems you may wish to consider as a starting point:

Alexander Pope: 'Epistle to Miss Blount, on her leaving the Town, after the Coronation' (1714)
William Wordsworth: extracts from *The Two-Part Prelude* (1799)
Gerard Manley Hopkins: 'Hurrahing in Harvest' (1877)
Ted Hughes: 'Rain' (1979)

Some anthologies to explore:

*The Rattle-Bag and The School Bag* ed. Hughes and Heaney
*The New Oxford Book of Romantic Verse* ed. McGann
*The New Oxford Book of English Verse* ed. Helen Gardner
*The Norton Anthology of Poetry*
*The New Golden Treasury of English Verse* ed. Leeson
*Caribbean Poetry Now* ed. Brow
*English Poetry Plus* Chadwyck-Healey (CD ROM)
*Project Gutenberg* Walnut Creek (CD ROM)
*Project Gutenberg* on the Internet (http: //www.promo.net/pg/

# Carol Ann Duffy | *IN MRS TILSCHER'S CLASS*

## PRELIMINARY STUDY

In this unit, and the three which follow, we'll explore some poems by a writer born in Glasgow in 1955. Each of the poems explores the writer's memories of childhood.

- What do you think the world was like when the writer was growing up? Think about anyone you know born about forty years ago. How do you think his/her childhood was similar to/different from yours?

- Talk about some of the ways you feel your outlook and your personality have changed since you left junior school. In what ways do you think you see yourself, other people and the world you live in differently from the way you saw them then?

  Do you think you can see yourself more clearly the further back you look? Why?

## CONCENTRATION EXERCISE

Get yourself comfortable. Close your eyes. Try to forget you're sitting in a classroom surrounded by others. For this exercise, you're on your own.

Here are some questions to think about in the secrecy of your private self. You won't have to share any of what you think about in the next few minutes with anyone else.

1 See if you can remember the name of somebody who taught you when you were about eleven years old.
2 Imagine yourself back in the school you went to then. Try to remember exactly what that particular teacher looked like – the eyes, the teeth, the lips, the hairstyle ...
3 What sort of clothes did s/he usually wear? See if you can visualise the shoes, the walk ...
4 Do you remember how s/he used to get to school? Alone or with somebody else; by car, on a bike, on a moped, on foot?
5 Did you know where your teacher lived?

6 Did s/he have any particular possessions which you still remember: a case; a watch; a ring; a badge; a pair of glasses? Try to picture one of those things so clearly that you could draw it.

7 See if you can remember how you used to feel when that teacher came into the room. Was s/he a comforting or a scary person?

8 Try to hear again in your head the way that teacher talked to the whole class. Was the voice loud, soft, gentle, musical or harsh? Did s/he have any favourite expressions? Did s/he have a distinctive accent?

9 Can you hear that teacher calling your name, talking to you? What about?  How does it make you feel? See if you can recall one particular thing that teacher said or did which amused, reassured, upset or irritated you.

10 Now think about what your lessons were like then. Try to remember one particular task you were asked to do. What pens, pencils, type of paper, equipment did you use? Was the task fun or hard work? Was it easy or confusing? What did you feel about doing it?

Jot down, as bullet points and in any order, as many of the things that you recalled as you can. Some things will be very particular: the smell of a cupboard perhaps; a peculiar picture on the wall. Other things may be more generalised: the taste of fun; the smell of fear.

Don't be over-fussy about presentation at this stage.

Remember that what everyone writes down is confidential.

## FIRST ASSIGNMENT

One hour

◆ Use your notes and the recollections which they trigger to write a piece called 'A Day in Mr/Mrs/Miss/Ms/Dr X's class'. You may write it as a short story or as a poem.

It will be up to you whether you write this for your own eyes only, or as a piece to share with others.

# In Mrs Tilscher's Class

You could travel up the Blue Nile
with your finger, tracing the route
while Mrs Tilscher chanted the scenery.
Tana. Ethiopia. Khartoum. Aswan.
That for a hour, then a skittle of milk
and the chalky Pyramids rubbed into dust.
A window opened with a long pole.
The laugh of a bell swung by a running child.

This was better than home. Enthralling books.
The classroom glowed like a sweetshop.
Sugar paper. Coloured shapes. Brady and Hindley
faded, like the faint, uneasy smudge of a mistake.
Mrs Tilscher loved you. Some mornings, you found
she'd left a good gold star by your name.
The scent of a pencil slowly, carefully, shaved.
A xylophone's nonsense heard from another form.

Over the Easter term, the inky tadpoles changed
from commas into exclamation marks. Three frogs
hopped in the playground, freed by a dunce,
followed by a line of kids, jumping and croaking
away from the lunch queue. A rough boy
told you how you were born. You kicked him, but stared
at your parents, appalled, when you got back home.

That feverish July, the air tasted of electricity.
A tangible alarm made you always untidy, hot,
fractious under the heavy, sexy sky. You asked her
how you were born and Mrs Tilscher smiled,
then turned away. Reports were handed out.
You ran through the gates, impatient to be grown,
as the sky split open into a thunderstorm.

## THINKING/TALKING POINTS

- Without looking back at the poem, discuss all the details that you remember. Here are some prompts:
    - what 'laughed'?
    - what did Mrs Tilscher sometimes leave by the speaker's name?

- what changed 'from commas into exclamation marks'?
- what did the 'rough boy' do? How did the speaker respond?

Now read through the poem again a couple of times.

- What do you like about the way some things are described?

- What does the poem remind you about from your junior school days? Which details in the poem described a world different from the one you grew up in? Discuss any details you didn't understand.

- What do you think the speaker meant when she described that particular July as 'feverish' and tasting 'of electricity'? Talk about how you remember your own last July at junior school.

  See if you can make up a phrase similar in style to Carol Ann Duffy's to capture the special flavour of those final days for you.

- At the end of the poem, the 'heavy, sexy sky' has given way to 'a thunderstorm'. What does that mean, *literally?* What do you think it means *figuratively?*

- 'You ran through the gates, impatient to be grown', How do you feel the real/imaginary gates of a primary school are like/unlike the gates of the school you're in now? How do you feel about the idea of running through those gates for the last time? Besides the school, what else will you leave behind?

  Now read or listen to the poem being read again a couple of times.

- Discuss anything new you noticed this time.

- How would you describe the speaker's tone of voice at different moments of the story?

- Pick out all the pleasant-sounding things in the first two stanzas. Where in the poem are pleasing-sounding things replaced by ugly things? Pick out the words which you feel alter the tone of the poem.

- How would you describe the mood of stanza four? Pick out the words you think create it.

- Describe the way you imagine Mrs Tilscher's smile. In what sense(s) do you think she 'turned away'? Why do you think she did that?

- Talk about what you liked in the poem. How was it similar to/different from the pieces you wrote?

## SECOND ASSIGNMENT

Choose one: two hours

◆ School Report
Imagine yourself as a newspaper reporter. You are writing a story about someone with your name and address and history who became famous. You visit his/her old primary school and meet his/her teacher.

Write a piece called *School Report* describing yourself as you think that teacher remembers you at eleven years old.
It might begin something like this:

> No. Not at all shy in those days. Not like when he arrived, little thumb-sucker. Quite a handful, Jo and Sam together. Nothing particular. Except I remember one afternoon, I walked into the classroom and ...

Or like this:

> Oh Vicki Parmenides! Remember her well.
> All hairspray and flounce at eleven!
> She'd bounce into the room
> Jabbering twenty to the dozen.

◆ 'In Ms/Mrs/Miss/Mr/Dr_____'s class'
Write your own poem modelled on Carol Ann Duffy's. Write four stanzas and use some of the language tricks you liked in Duffy's poem. See if you can make it exactly the same length.

◆ Exploring Carol Ann Duffy's Poem 'In Mrs Tilscher's Class'
Write an essay examining the poem. Begin by describing what you think Carol Ann Duffy set out to do. Then pick out half a dozen details you particularly liked, quote them and talk about what made them interesting/amusing/powerful. Finally, discuss whether you think the speaker simply feels nostalgic about her old school or sees leaving it as something positive.

## FOR FURTHER STUDY

**Poems**
Seamus Heaney: 'Death of a Naturalist'
Dylan Thomas: 'Fern Hill'
William Wordsworth: 'The Two-Part Prelude'

**Novels**
Ethel Richardson: *The Getting of Wisdom* (also a film)
Jeanette Winterson: *Oranges are Not the Only Fruit*
S E Hinton: *The Outsiders; That Was Then This Is Now; Rumble Fish* (all also films)
Barry Hines: *A Kestrel for a Knave* (also a film)
J D Salinger: *The Catcher in the Rye*
James Joyce: *Portrait of the Artist as a Young Man*
Charles Dickens: *David Copperfield* (also a film)
Henry James: *What Maisie Knew*

**Short stories**
Dylan Thomas: *Portrait of the Artist as a Young Dog*

**Films**
*If ...* directed by Lindsay Anderson
*Dead Poets' Society* directed by Peter Weir

**Radio Play**
Dylan Thomas: *Return Journey*

# Carol Ann Duffy | THE CAPTAIN OF THE 1964 TOP OF THE FORM TEAM

## PRELIMINARY ASSIGNMENT: THE ARCHAEOLOGIST, THE REPORT AND THE REFUTATION

In pairs: two hours

◆ An archaeologist is someone who digs up the past – or what's left of it. From the fragments an archaeologist finds, s/he tries to make sense of the generations which came before.

Imagine that in a few thousand years' time, an archaeologist is ferreting around the buried remains of your family home. The one so spectacularly covered by millions of tons of earth when a meteorite the size of Barnsley collided with Earth in November 2009.

The human remains (the lower half of your skeleton, two and a half teeth and some strands of hair) are pretty much like all the other human remains which our archaeologist has unearthed elsewhere. But what interests the archaeologist is the particular collection of artefacts s/he's discovered which make your house and, more particularly, your room unique.

Other people of your generation had some of the same things. But not one of them had the precise combination of things, valuable and cheap, mass-produced and hand-made, unearthed near your bones.

Cloning the long-disappeared from bits of recovered DNA has long since been discredited. However, the archaeologist believes that, s/he can 'reconstruct' your lifestyle, your habits, likes and loathings, achievements and failures, pains and ambitions from the bits and pieces salvaged from your room.

So we don't have to wait a few thousand years for the excavation to be undertaken, we'd like you to compile **The Archaeologist's File**. It will consist first of **The Catalogue** of the things found in your room, in your 'sector of the home-territory', as it is rather quaintly termed in the journal *Archaeologist's Review*.

What follows will be **The Archaeologist's Report** in which s/he boldly goes beyond what can be certain into speculating about the way you behaved, what you ate at various times of the day, what you valued and worshipped, what you used to ward off evil and to ensure your fellow earthlings admired, desired, or even worshipped you. Use a suitably academic register in which to write your report. You will find some examples of that kind of language in the entries below.

The trouble is that another archaeologist has got possession of the catalogue too. His/her report presents a very different set of conclusions from the same evidence. **The Refutation** as it is known, describes a person feared and disliked, even by members of your own family, at war with society and with your close friends, and driven by crazy ambitions. According to The Refutation, if the meteorite hadn't struck, you would have caused an even greater geodisaster ...

### 1 The Catalogue

Here you list (perhaps with accompanying photographs/sketches) the various objects, some intact, others in fragments, discovered in the rubble of your 'sector of the home-territory'. It might look something like this:

```
Artefacts


implement with plastic and steel teeth
set in rubber cushion (handle missing?)


two hundred digitally encoded, optically-readable
discs, storing bewildering variety of
unintelligible human and non-human noises


large pile of decorated paper sheets, of many
different sizes and designs, stitched
or glued into elaborately-decorated folders


metal box of short wooden arrows tipped
with graphite


box engraved with signs 'JR 4 FG'
and 'Well Wicked'


box also contained figurine of nude male
modelled in plastic-putty compound
```

Swap your files and then follow the instructions below.

## 2 The Archaeologist's Report

Alongside each entry, make some tentative suggestions of what the artefact may have been used for. For example:

---

<u>Artefacts</u>

*Probable function*

implement with plastic and steel teeth
set in rubber cushion (handle missing?)

*delousing the hair*

two hundred digitally encoded, optically-readable
discs, storing bewildering variety of
unintelligible human and non-human noises

*intruder deterrents?*
*variety of noises suited to*
*scare off variety of rivals/pests*

large pile of decorated paper sheets, of many
different sizes and designs, stitched
or glued into elaborately-decorated folders

*evidence of toilet fetish*
*clearly considerable care*
*expended upon the*
*manufacture of lavatory paper*

metal box of short wooden arrows tipped
with graphite

*primitive black magic*
*ceremonial casque*

box engraved with signs 'JR 4 FG'
and 'Well Wicked'

box also contained figurine of nude male
modelled in plastic-putty compound

---

## 3 The Archaeologist's Findings and The Refutation

Both of these documents attempt to present to the world of the year 3007 a picture of the person you were, the life you led. The first uses the evidence from The Catalogue to paint you in an attractive light, as something of a celebrity or at least a decent, fully-functional citizen. The second uses the same evidence to prove what an anti-social beast lurked behind those respectable-looking curtains at 17, Foxglove Avenue, Lavender Roding, ... (supply your own address).

# The Captain of the 1964 Top of the Form Team

*Do Wah Diddy Diddy, Baby Love, Oh Pretty Woman*
were in the Top Ten that month, October, and the Beatles
were everywhere else. I can give you the B-side
of the Supremes one. Hang on. *Come See About Me?*
I lived in a kind of fizzing hope. Gargling
with Vimto. The clever smell of my satchel. Convent girls.
I pulled my hair forward with a steel comb that I blew
like Mick, my lips numb as a two-hour snog.

No snags. The Nile rises in April. Blue and White.
The humming-bird's song is made by its wings, which beat
so fast that they blur in flight. I knew the capitals,
the Kings and Queens, the dates. In class, the white sleeve
of my shirt saluted again and again. *Sir! ... Correct.*
Later, I whooped at the side of my bike, a cowboy,
mounted it running in one jump. I sped down Dyke Hill,
no hands, famous, learning, *dominus domine dominum.*

*Dave Dee Dozy* ... Try me. Come on. My mother kept my
    mascot Gonk
on the TV set for a year. And the photograph. I look
so brainy you'd think I'd just had a bath. The blazer.
The badge. The tie. The first chord of *A Hard Day's Night*
loud in my head. I ran to the Spinney in my prize shoes,
up Churchill Way, up Nelson Drive, over pink pavements
that girls chalked on, in a blue evening; and I stamped
the paw prints of badgers and skunks in the mud. My
    country.

I want it back. The Captain. The one with all the answers.
    *Bzz.*
My name was in red on Lucille Green's jotter. I smiled
as wide as a child who went missing on the way home
from school. The keeny. I say to my stale wife
*Six hits by Dusty Springfield.* I say to my boss *A pint!*
*How can we know the dancer from the dance?* Nobody.
My thick kids wince. *Name the Prime Minister of Rhodesia.*
My country. *How many florins in a pound?*

## THINKING/TALKING POINTS

- Do you think Carol Ann Duffy's poem is a bit like an archaeologist's catalogue? Why?

- Before you listen to or read the piece for a second time, jot down a) any of the items the speaker mentions that you can remember, and b) your first impression of the person to whom these memories were so precious.

  Now read or listen to the poem again.

  Are there a few more details you can make sense of?

- Can you sing any of the songs? Do you have any idea what a B-side was – or a satchel? Who was Mick?

- What did that odd phrase 'dominus domine dominum' suggest to you? What was the Bzz? And a jotter? How many florins in a pound?

## SECOND ASSIGNMENT

**In pairs: thirty minutes**

Divide a sheet of A4 paper into two columns. Head one 'Artefact', the other 'Description'.

- Read through the poem together a few times and then make a list of all the different things from the past the speaker mentions. Alongside each one write as clear a description of the thing as you can. If you have no idea what the thing referred to is, see if you can come up with a plausible (or, even better, funny) explanation.

  See if you can work out why the poem has the strange title it does.

## THIRD ASSIGNMENT

**In groups: one hour**

- This poem is about communication – or non-communication. It's about the way it's difficult for one generation to understand another.

  Talk about why this is true now. Why a great deal of the language your parents use needs to be 'translated' before you can understand it. Why your parents are baffled by some of the words you use every day.

## IN TWO GROUPS

◆ Group one: *The Oldspeak Dictionary*
See how many words you can come up with which are in the process of leaving the language. They may be words your parents or grandparents still use, but which aren't part of your usual vocabulary. For example, who do you know who talks about the following?

| | | | |
|---|---|---|---|
| pennies | the Iron Curtain | telegrams | the permanent way |
| a hearth rug | an usherette | Spam | a put-u-up |
| a bad egg | Belisha beacons | gallons | the gramophone |
| blighters | the spin drier | snaps | dentifrice |
| railway engines | anthracite | a pal | the wireless |
| the never-never | the rates | nip | goose pimples |

See how many of the words in this list you can define. Add as many other obsolete words and their definitions as you can.

Present all your findings as the first edition of the *Oldspeak Dictionary*. Look at the conventions various dictionaries use to present their materials and use the one you find most readable.

◆ Group two: *The Newspeak Dictionary*
See how many words and phrases you can come up with which have come into general use (or have begun to be used in new ways) since you started to talk. For example, your parents probably didn't use any of these words or phrases when they were your age:

| | | | | |
|---|---|---|---|---|
| CD ROM | surfing the net | digitise | epilator | chicksticks |
| vegeburger | eyewear | chunnel | email | feisty |
| satellite dish | scam | geek | anorexia | minidisc |
| millenium bug | goosebumps | fragrance | nuke | digitise |

When they used the following words, they may have meant something different from what you mean when you use them:

| | | | | |
|---|---|---|---|---|
| coke | wicked | cassette | rave | spectacles |
| pc | ticker | @ | ecstasy | processor |
| compatible | money | analogue | monitor | sad |
| eat | facial | cool | out of order | gay |
| server | tragic | web | tubby | gas |

See how many of the words in the last list you can define in at least two different ways. Then add as many examples of newly-minted or refurbished words as you can, with their definitions.

Present all your findings as the first edition of the *Newspeak Dictionary*. Look at the conventions various dictionaries use to present their materials and use the one you find most readable.

## FOURTH ASSIGNMENT

*Two hours: choose one*

Read through Carol Ann Duffy's poem a few more times. Then write one of the following.

◆ Just talking: a playscript for two actors
The scene is a home for the elderly in the late 2070's.
You and a friend talk about old times: growing up in the late nineties and the early years of the century. You compare that easy, safe, familiar world to the bewildering place you find yourselves in now.

You're surprised how many things have changed. Things you used to be able to buy are no longer available or don't taste, work, feel like they used to. The language has changed so much too. Often your grandchildren laugh because your words are quaint or mean all sorts of things to them that you didn't intend.

◆ Write a poem modelled closely upon 'The Captain of the 1964 Top of the Form Team'. See if you can find contemporary equivalents for each of the sixties' references in Duffy's poem. Try to convey to the reader how terribly sad, how long past your sell-by date you will seem in seventy years' time.

Close your eyes. Think back. One day something happened which you'll never forget. It may be something you've never told anyone else about. To talk about it would be embarrassing, too complicated, perhaps, to explain properly to someone who wasn't there, who wasn't you.

Now listen to or read carefully the following poem a couple of times.

## Stafford Afternoons

Only there, the afternoons could suddenly pause
and when I looked up from lacing my shoe
a long road held no one, the gardens were empty,
an ice-cream van chimed and dwindled away.

On the motorway bridge, I waved at windscreens,
oddly hurt by the blurred waves back, the speed.
So I let a horse in the noisy field sponge at my palm
and invented, in colour, a vivid lie for us both.

In a cul-de-sac, a strange boy threw a stone.
I crawled through a hedge into long grass
at the edge of a small wood, lonely and thrilled.
The green silence gulped once and swallowed me whole.

I knew it was dangerous. The way the trees
drew sly faces from light and shade, the wood
let out its sticky breath on the back of my neck,
and flowering nettles gathered spit in their throats.

Too late. *Touch*, said the long-haired man
who stood, legs apart, by a silver birch
with a living, purple root in his hand. The sight
made sound rush back; birds, a distant lawnmower,

his hoarse, frightful endearments as I backed away
then ran all the way home; into a game
where  children scattered and shrieked
and time fell from the sky like a red ball.

## THINKING/TALKING POINTS

On your own:
ten minutes

- Imagine that what you've just heard was a story someone told you, in whispers, in confidence, some weeks ago. Now the storyteller has gone missing. The girl's family is desperate. They have asked everyone who knew her to help the police with their enquiries.

  All you can think of is that story – but you can't remember all the details. You're not even sure what some of the details meant. But the story may suggest why/how/where the girl disappeared. You must try to recall as much as possible. The tiniest fragment may provide a vital clue.

  Jot down, as bullet points, whatever you can recall of that whispered confidence.

In small groups:
thirty minutes

- Take it in turns to tell each other what you remember of the girl's story. See if between you, you can remember her exact words, even where it's likely she didn't fully understand what was going on. Then discuss what you think happened.

- Nominate a spokesman to present what your group made of the girl's story to the rest of the class.

- Discuss your findings. What lines of enquiry might the police now follow up?

- Now listen to or read the poem again. Do you think anything you'd forgotten or misunderstood is significant?

## ASSIGNMENT

Two hours: choose one

- ◆ Read through the poem a few times, trying to imagine yourself in the girl's place at each point in the story. What we have here are just a few details of the dozens of things she must have seen, heard and felt.

  For example, when she was on the bridge over the motorway, she would have noticed lots of different cars, lorries. She'd have heard the roar the traffic made and the occasional silences. She'd have smelt the diesel fumes from an old lorry, perhaps.

  When she reached the edge of the small wood, were there any dandelions in bloom? Were there brambles which scratched her legs?

Did she almost twist her ankle in a rabbit hole? Did she hear the sound of a tractor working the next field? Did the grass smell sweet or sour?

That man – did she notice anything else at all about him? His eyes? How tall, how thin or heavy he was? Was he wearing a hat, glasses, a smart city suit, a shabby tracksuit?

When she got back, which children were playing in the street?

When you have worked on different parts of the poem in this way, re-present the whole poem as a short story. It could be written in the first person, like this:

> Yes I remember it. All too clearly. Everyone else had gone to see the Red Twins' film. It was a lovely August afternoon and I was enjoying being free to wander on my own ...

It could be in the third person, like this:

> She knew what people said about Bates's Field, but it was her special place. The place she went to be alone, to think, to dream and make up wonderful adventures ...

◆ Read through the poem a few times to see how Carol Ann Duffy has begun by setting the scene, then moved to the crisis and then quickly brought the story to an end.

Look at the way the poet's language shows the girl's mood at different moments in the story.

Use the poem as a template in which to tell a story of your own. It may be about something which really happened to you, something you've heard or read about, or just made up. Try to use the same number of lines in each stanza as Duffy has, and to keep the rhythm and tempo steady.

You may like to write a commentary on your poem, describing how it is like/unlike 'Stafford Afternoons'. Quote half a dozen details from Duffy's poem and from your own in your commentary.

# Carol Ann Duffy | *LITANY*

## THINKING/TALKING POINTS

Every community has its own way of saying things, its own language. Some communities are as big as a country, some as small as a couple. Most of us speak several languages, even if we don't speak a foreign language.

• Discuss these ideas. Do you think they are true? Why?

• What different languages do you speak? Describe some of the ways they differ from each other.

Imagine yourself curled up in an armchair, trying to read the newspaper. The phone rings and someone in the house answers. Without listening carefully to the half-conversation going on in the next room, you know who's talking – not just on your end of the line but on the other end too.

• Do you think this is true? If you were listening to someone in your house talking on the phone, would you know whether the person on the other end was a particular member of the family, a friend, one of the neighbours, a stranger, the person who fixes the car, or a teacher ringing up to see why you weren't in school? How?

## FIRST ASSIGNMENT

◆ The telephone rings four times. Each time it's answered by the same person – somebody you live with. You can hear only one half of the conversations. Each time, the person talking at your end of the line talks differently – because the person at the other end of the line is someone different: not just someone with a different name but someone with a different relationship to the person a few feet away from you.

Write four different half-conversations, showing how we pick up clues to let us know who each caller is. For example, here are sketches of four different sorts of half-conversations. Think about the ways they are different.

| One | Two | Three | Four |
|---|---|---|---|
| 37946 | 3794... | Hello. 37946 | 37946 |
| Oh, hi! Great! ... | Yes. | Yes, it's Mrs Robins | Look, I've had just |
| Yes, it's just arrived. | Yes. | speaking. | about enough of you. |
|  |  |  |  |
| Perfect! You're very | Yes but I told.. | Oh, yes. I did | No. You can't. |
| clever, I've searched |  | receive your |  |
| for one everywhere. | No. | message but I | She's busy. |
|  | No! | was late back from | Doing her homework |
| No, pet, don't worry. | | work so it was too |  |
| I'll speak to Mum | You... Did...? | late to telephone | She does her home- |
| about it.. She was | OK | you yesterday... | work first! |
| just a bit upset... |  |  |  |
|  | Bye, I'll... |  | No. You |
|  |  |  | are not her homework! |
|  | Typical! |  |  |
|  |  |  | Cocky bugger! |

When you write your conversations, you may like to leave larger or shorter gaps between each contribution to show how much/how little of each conversation the speaker at your end provides/controls.

Here's a piece exploring, among other things, the language a child was surrounded by at home. Listen to or read it a couple of times. Then jot down your impression of the people in the child's house.

## Litany

The soundtrack then was a litany – *candlewick
bedspread three piece suite display cabinet* –
and stiff-haired wives balanced their red smiles,
passing the catalogue. *Pyrex.* A tiny ladder
ran up Mrs Barr's American Tan leg, sly
like a rumour. Language embarrassed them.

The terrible marriages crackled, cellophane
round polyester shirts, and then The Lounge
would seem to bristle with eyes, hard
as the bright stones in engagement rings,

and sharp hands poised over biscuits as a word
was spelled out. An embarrassing word, broken

to bits, which tensed the air like an accident.
This was the code I learnt at my mother's knee, pretending
to read, where no one had cancer, or sex, or debts,
and certainly not leukaemia, which no one could spell.
The year a mass grave of wasps bobbed in a jam-jar;
a butterfly stammered itself in my curious hands.

*A boy in the playground*, I said, *told me
to fuck off;* and a thrilled, malicious pause
salted my tongue like an imminent storm. Then
uproar. *I'm sorry, Mrs Barr, Mrs Hunt, Mrs Emery,
sorry, Mrs Raine.* Yes, I can summon their names.
My mother's mute shame. The taste of soap.

## THINKING/TALKING ABOUT LANGUAGE

- Look at this detail:

                    A tiny ladder
    ran up Mrs Barr's American Tan leg, sly
    like a rumour.

What sort of language is the phrase 'American Tan'? What do you think it
means? Where in that room would you be likely to find the word printed?
What other words in the first stanza come from the same source?

- What connotations do the words 'American Tan' have for you? For
  example, do you think the phrase suggests any of the following:
  | | | | |
  |---|---|---|---|
  | poverty | chic | elegance | confidence |
  | edginess | loneliness | money | sleaze |

- What impression of Mrs Barr does the phrase 'Mrs Barr's American Tan
  leg' convey to you?

- How is that impression changed by the other details:

                    A tiny ladder
    ran up Mrs Barr's American Tan leg, sly
    like a rumour.

- In lines 7–8 comes this:

> The terrible marriages crackled, cellophane
> round polyester shirts,

What does the word 'crackles' usually mean? If you had been in the room, what would you have heard literally crackling?

What do you think the women were saying and feeling about their marriages?

Talk about the phrase 'The terrible marriages crackled'. See if you can explain how Duffy has played with language to create a powerful way of presenting the atmosphere the child sensed.

- Close your eyes and try to picture your mother's hands. Think of some words and phrases to describe them. Jot them down. Talk about the impression of their mothers different people in the class convey, simply by the ways they describe their mother's hands.

  How does the speaker in the poem describe the hands of the women in the room? Why is that such a curious way to describe hands? Talk about how effective you find it. What impression of the women does it convey?

- When the speaker says that nobody could spell 'leukaemia', she could mean two rather different things.
  What do you think is the *literal* meaning of the sentence? And the *figurative?*

- Imagine a butterfly. Jot down as many words as you can think of to suggest the way it behaves and the way seeing one makes you feel.

  Look at the moment in the poem when the speaker recalls trapping a butterfly. Comment on the language Duffy uses to describe the episode. What do you find interesting about her choice of words?

- Read lines 19–21 in the final stanza again. See if you can explain in a scientific, analytic way exactly why the words the girl repeated had the effect they did at this gathering but had a completely different effect when the boy used them.

  Talk about your own experiences of a 'storm' brewed by an unconventional use of language.

## SECOND ASSIGNMENT

Two hours: choose one

◆ Exploring language-play

Read through a selection of poems from any anthology. Make a study of three or four, including this one if you wish, in which the poet has deliberately used words in unexpected ways to achieve interesting effects.

For each example you quote, explain as carefully as you can what games have been played with meaning, syntax, grammar and/or lexis and the way this has made the language rich in meaning, flexible, interesting, subtle or simply memorable. Have you found any examples of language-play where you feel the effect is clever but not entirely successful? If so explain why you think the trick has backfired.

◆ Poetry appreciation

Write a detailed study of 'Litany', examining carefully the way the poet has recreated the atmosphere and the experiences of the child in that particular community on that particular day.

Pick out six or seven details which you think are particularly powerful. Explain what you think each of them means and describe how they work. For example, as well as the ones we have examined, you might want to talk about some of these phrases:

The soundtrack then was a litany

stiff-haired wives balanced their red smiles

The Lounge would ... bristle with eyes, hard as the bright stones in engagement rings

What attitude to Mrs Barr, Mrs Hunt, Mrs Emery and Mrs Raine do you think the poet expects us to have? Explain why you think that. How do you think we are meant to feel about the child and the mother?

◆ Creative response

Using 'Litany' as a model, write your own poem. Try to make your piece similar in shape and length to Duffy's.
In your poem, explore part of the world you grew up in.
Try to give the reader/listener a strong impression of the people who surrounded you, of 'the code' by which they lived, and of your own feelings at the time and of the way you feel about your past now.

Use scraps of conversation as Duffy has. And also some sharp, descriptive phrases similar to 'The year a mass grave of wasps bobbed in a jam-jar'.

# Wordsworth | *LUCY GRAY* and *FIVE LYRICS*

# Ian McEwan | from *THE CHILD IN TIME*

## THINKING/TALKING POINTS

# Frantic father's hopes fade

In pairs/small groups

- Suggest and discuss various stories you might find under this headline in a popular newspaper.

- Talk about the kind of language *(lexis)* used in tabloid journalism. What reaction to this story do you think a reporter would hope to get from the readers? How would the language used help to achieve such a reaction? For example, which of these words do you think would be appropriate to this style of journalism?

*To describe the father and his feelings:*

| | | | |
|---|---|---|---|
| distraught | apprehensive | despondent | hysterical |
| gob-smacked | anxious | tortured | distressed |
| devastated | gutted | inconsolable | crazy |
| wan | exhausted | bereft | forlorn |
| well-scared | knackered | berserk | tearful |
| haggard | shocked | irate | |

*To describe the missing child:*

| | | | |
|---|---|---|---|
| tot | tiny | blue-eyed | trusting |
| mite | vulnerable | debonair | bolshy |
| young person | accomplished | fun-loving | precocious |
| child | talented | plucky | retiring |
| kiddy | easy-going | popular | shy |
| infant | unflappable | gregarious | |
| diminutive | extrovert | naive | |

*To describe the scene, the search, people's speculations:*

| | | | |
|---|---|---|---|
| enquiry | exhaustive | fruitless | weirdo |
| hunt | painstaking | horrific | indigent |
| search | dour | playground | down and out |
| quiz | harrowing | kindergarten | enigma |
| interrogation | abortive | teddy-bear | mystery |

Add your own choice of appropriate words to those you have chosen from these lists.

### PRELIMINARY ASSIGNMENT

One hour

◆ You are a reporter for *The Daily Mirror*, writing a short article on the story line above. You have a limit of two hundred and fifty words and one hour in which to draft, proof read and redraft your piece, ready for printing.

When it's complete, display your article alongside those that other people have produced. Discuss the different ways the story has been presented, looking at:
  – content
  – tone
  – lexis
  – sentence and paragraph structure
  – layout/typography.

## Lucy Gray; Or, Solitude

Oft I had heard of Lucy Gray:
And, when I crossed the wild,
I chanced to see at break of day
The solitary child.

No mate, no comrade Lucy knew;
She dwelt on a wide moor,
- The sweetest thing that ever grew
Beside a human door!

You yet may spy the fawn at play,
The hare upon the green;
But the sweet face of Lucy Gray
Will never more be seen.

'To-night will be a stormy night –
You to the town must go;
And take a lantern, Child, to light
Your mother through the snow.'

'That, Father! will I gladly do:
'Tis scarcely afternoon –
The minster-clock has just struck two,
And yonder is the moon!'

**faggot:** a bundle of firewood

At this the father raised his hook,
And snapped a faggot-band;
He plied his work; – and Lucy took
The lantern in her hand.

**blither:** happier
**roe:** deer
**wanton:** free and easy

Not blither is the mountain roe;
With many a wanton stroke
Her feet disperse the powdery snow,
That rises up like smoke.

The storm came on before its time: ·
She wandered up and down;
And many a hill did Lucy climb:
But never reached the town.

The wretched parents all that night
Went shouting far and wide;
But there was neither sound nor sight
To serve them for a guide.

At day-break on a hill they stood
That overlooked the moor;
And thence they saw the bridge of wood,
A furlong from their door.

**furlong:** 220 yards

They wept – and, turning homeward, cried,
'In heaven we all shall meet,'
– When in the snow the mother spied
The print of Lucy's feet.

Then downwards from the steep hill's edge
They tracked the footmarks small;
And through the broken hawthorn hedge,
And by the long stone-wall;

And then an open field they crossed:
The marks were still the same;
They tracked them on, nor ever lost;
And to the bridge they came.

They followed from the snowy bank
Those footmarks, one by one,
Into the middle of the plank;
And further there were none!
– Yet some maintain that to this day
She is a living child;
That you may see sweet Lucy Gray
Upon the lonesome wild.

O'er rough and smooth she trips along,
And never looks behind;
And sings a solitary song
That whistles in the wind.

## THINKING/TALKING POINTS

• Does this poem sound to you as though it was written recently or some time ago? Jot down reasons why you feel the way you do.

• Here are some dates. Which of these do you feel is closest to the time when 'Lucy Gray' was written? Why?

| | |
|---|---|
| 1400 | The last of Chaucer's *Canterbury Tales* was written |
| 1600 | Shakespeare's *Henry V* was staged for the first time |
| 18th century | Picture a) opposite was produced |
| 19th century | Picture b) opposite was produced |
| 1914–18 | Wilfred Owen's war poems were written |
| 1946 | The first atomic bomb was dropped on Hiroshima |
| 1994 | Microsoft's *Encarta* was published on CD ROM |

a) Nathaniel Dance: 'The Misses Tracy-Travell'

b) Sophie Anderson: 'Returning Home from School'

## SECOND ASSIGNMENT

One hour

◆ The poem could include some extra lines, describing what Lucy's parents said to each other while they were searching for her. Read the poem again, thinking about where these lines would fit best.

Write the addition to the poem. It could be four or eight lines long. Make a fair copy of your lines and share them with the rest of the group. Discuss what you think works best in your different versions and why.

# From *The Child in Time*

Listen to or read through the following extract a couple of times. It is from the novel *The Child in Time* by Ian McEwan.

It was a two-minute walk to the supermarket, over the four-lane road by a zebra crossing. Near where they waited to cross was a motor-bike salesroom, an international meeting place for bikers. Melon-bellied men in worn leathers leaned against or sat astride their stationary machines. When Kate withdrew the knuckle she had been sucking and pointed, the low sun illuminated a smoking finger. However, she found no word to frame what she saw. They crossed at last, in front of an impatient pack of cars which snarled forwards the moment they reached the centre island. Kate looked out for the lollipop lady, the one who always recognised her. Stephen explained it was Saturday. There were crowds, he held her hand tightly as they moved towards the entrance. Amid voices, shouts, the electro-mechanical rattle at the checkout counters, they found a trolley. Kate was smiling hugely to herself as she made herself comfortable in her seat.

The people who used the supermarket divided into two groups, as distinct as tribes or nations. The first lived locally in modernised Victorian terraced houses which they owned. The second lived locally in tower blocks and council estates. Those in the first group tended to buy fresh fruit and vegetables, brown bread, coffee beans, fresh fish from a special counter, wine and spirits, while those in the second group bought tinned or frozen vegetables, baked beans, instant soup, white sugar, cupcakes, beer, spirits and cigarettes. In the second group were pensioners buying meat for their cats, biscuits for themselves. And there were young mothers, gaunt with fatigue, their mouths set hard round cigarettes, who sometimes cracked at the checkout and gave a child a spanking. In the first group were young, childless couples, flamboyantly dressed, who at worst were a little pressed for time. There were also mothers shopping with their au pairs, and fathers like Stephen, buying fresh salmon, doing their bit.

What else did he buy? Toothpaste, tissues, washing-up liquid, and best bacon, a leg of lamb, steak, green and red peppers, radice, potatoes, tin foil, a litre of Scotch. And who was there when his hand reached for these items? Someone who followed him as he pushed Kate along the stacked aisles, who stood a few paces off when he stopped, who pretended to be interested in a label and then continued when he did? He had been back a thousand times, seen his own hand, a shelf, the goods accumulate, heard Kate chattering on, and tried to move his eyes, lift them against the weight of time, to find that shrouded figure at the periphery of vision, the one who was always to the side and slightly behind, who, filled with a strange desire, was calculating odds, or simply waiting. But time held his sight for ever on his mundane errands, and all about him shapes without definition drifted and dissolved, lost to categories.

Fifteen minutes later they were at the checkout. There were eight parallel counters. He joined a small queue nearest the door because he knew the girl at the till worked fast. There were three people ahead of him when he stopped the trolley and there was no one behind him when he turned to lift Kate from her seat. She was enjoying herself and was reluctant to be disturbed. She whined and hooked her foot into her seat. He had to lift her high to get her clear. He noted her irritability with absent-minded satisfaction – it was a sure sign of her tiredness. By the time this little struggle was over, there were two people ahead of them, one of whom was about to leave. He came round to the front of the trolley to unload it on to the conveyor belt. Kate was holding on to the wide bar at the other end of the trolley, pretending to push. There was no one behind her. Now the person immediately ahead of Stephen, a man with a curved back, was about to pay for several tins of dog food. Stephen lifted the first items on to the belt. When he straightened he might have been conscious of a figure in a dark coat behind Kate. But it was hardly an awareness at all, it was the weakest suspicion brought to life by a desperate memory. The coat could have been a dress or a shopping bag or his own invention. He was intent on ordinary tasks, keen to finish them. He was barely a conscious being at all.

The man with the dog food was leaving. The checkout girl was already at work, the fingers of one hand flickering over the keypad while the other drew Stephen's items towards her. As he took the salmon from the trolley he glanced down at Kate and winked. She copied him, but clumsily, wrinkling her nose and closing both eyes. He set the fish down and asked the girl for a carrier bag. She reached under a shelf and pulled one out. He took it and turned. Kate was gone. There was no one in the queue behind him. Unhurriedly he pushed the trolley clear, thinking she had ducked down behind the end of the counter. Then he took a few paces and glanced down the only aisle she would have had time to reach. He stepped back and looked to his left and right. On one side there were lines of shoppers, on the other a clear space, then the chrome turnstile, then the automatic doors on to the pavement. There may have been a figure in a coat hurrying away from him, but at that time Stephen was looking for a three-year-old child, and his immediate worry was the traffic.

This was a theoretical, precautionary anxiety. As he shouldered past shoppers and emerged on to the broad pavement he knew he would not see her there. Kate was not adventurous in this way. She was not a strayer. She was too sociable, she preferred the company of the one she was with. She was also terrified of the road. He turned back and relaxed. She had to be in the shop, and she could come to no real harm there. He expected to see her emerging from behind the lines of shoppers at the checkouts. It was easy enough to overlook a child in the first flash of concern, to look too hard, too quickly. Still, a sickness and a tightening at the base of the throat, an unpleasant lightness in the feet, were with him as he went back. When he walked past all the tills, ignoring the girl at his who was irritably trying to attract his attention, a chill rose to the top of his stomach. At a controlled run – he was not yet past caring how foolish he looked – he went down all the aisles, past mountains of oranges, toilet rolls, soup. It was not until he was back at his starting point that he abandoned all propriety, filled his constricted lungs and shouted Kate's name.

Now he was taking long strides, bawling her name as he pounded the length of an aisle and headed once more for the door. Faces were turning towards him. There was no mistaking him for one of the drunks who blundered in to buy cider. His fear was too evident, too forceful, it filled the impersonal, fluorescent space with unignorable human warmth. Within moments all shopping around him had ceased. Baskets and trolleys were set aside, people were converging and saying Kate's name and somehow, in no time at all, it was generally known that she was three, that she was last seen at the checkout, that she wore green dungarees and carried a toy donkey. The faces of mothers were strained, alert. Several people had seen the little girl riding in the trolley. Someone knew the colour of her sweater. The anonymity of the city store turned out to be frail, a thin crust beneath which people observed, judged, remembered. A group of shoppers surrounding Stephen moved towards the door. At his side was the girl from the checkout, her face rigid with intent. There were other members of the supermarket hierarchy in brown coats, white coats, blue suits, who suddenly were no longer warehousemen or sub-managers or company representatives, but fathers, potential or real. They were all out on the pavement now, some crowding round Stephen asking questions or offering consolation while others, more usefully, set off in different directions to look in the doorways of nearby shops.

The lost child was everyone's property. But Stephen was alone. He looked through and beyond the kindly faces pressing in. They were irrelevant. Their voices did not reach him, they were impediments to his field of vision. They were blocking his view of Kate. He had to swim through them, push them aside to get to her. He had no air, he could not think. He heard himself pronounce the word 'stolen' and the word was taken up and spread to the peripheries, to passersby who were drawn to the commotion. The tall girl with the fast fingers who had looked so strong was crying. Stephen had time to feel momentary disappointment in her. As if summoned by the word he had spoken, a white police car spattered with mud cruised to a halt at the kerb. Official confirmation of disaster made him nauseous. Something was rising in his throat and he bent double. Perhaps he was sick, but he had no memory of it. The next thing was the supermarket again, and this time rules of appropriateness, of social order had selected the people at his side – a manager, a young woman who might have been a personal assistant, a sub-manager and two policemen. It was suddenly quiet.

## COMPARING TEXTS

- Discuss the various ways in which this extract is similar to/different from the poem.

**In pairs/small groups**

In your points for discussion you may wish to consider the following:
- the way the two stories are narrated
- the storytellers' tones of voice
- the details given in each which help us imagine where and when the story is set
- your feelings about the two children, and about the parents in each of the stories.

## THIRD ASSIGNMENT

Choose one: two hours

◆ Reread the McEwan extract a couple of times. Then in small groups improvise the action as a short play, inventing suitable dialogue.

◆ Read the extract a few times, making notes on the way it is written: the kind of language the writer uses; the style and structure of sentences and paragraphs; the vocabulary used; the narrator's changing tone of voice.

Write three or four paragraphs which might follow on from the extract you have read. Concentrate upon maintaining the *style* and *mood* of the original. Don't try to bring the story to an abrupt, easy 'end': leave your reader wanting to hear more.

◆ Re-present the story as if someone else were telling it. That person could be:
a) the girl at the checkout
b) one of the customers in the store
c) the child
d) a man or woman responsible for the child's disappearance
e) one of the police officers.

Remember that your storyteller may have seen lots of different things from the original narrator. S/he may notice other things or describe them in a different way. Your storyteller may be more or less reliable than the first. The way you tell the story may show the father in a different light from the way he comes across in Ian McEwan's version.

◆ Working individually or in pairs, use the material from *The Child in Time* and reshape it so it is similar to Wordsworth's 'Lucy Gray'. Think about the shape of each stage of the story, the use of rhythm and rhyme, and the point of view from which you wish to present it.

When you have completed your piece, you may wish to write a commentary, explaining what you were trying to do and how you went about it. Quote from the poem, the novel and from your own piece in your commentary.

After writing, present your pieces to each other and discuss how stories work when told in different ways.

# Five lyrics by Wordsworth

In 1799, Wordsworth published five other poems about the loss of someone called Lucy.

(i)

Strange fits of passion have I known:
And I will dare to tell,
But in the Lover's ear alone,
What once to me befell.

When she I loved looked every day
Fresh as a rose in June,
I to her cottage bent my way,
Beneath an evening moon.

**lea:** open countryside

**nigh:** near to

Upon the moon I fixed my eye,
All over the wide lea;
With quickening pace my horse drew nigh
Those paths so dear to me.

And now we reached the orchard-plot;
And, as we climbed the hill,
The sinking moon to Lucy's cot
Came near, and nearer still.

**boon:** gift

In one of those sweet dreams I slept,
Kind Nature's gentlest boon!
And all the while my eyes I kept
On the descending moon.

My horse moved on; hoof after hoof
He raised, and never stopped:
When down behind the cottage roof,
At once, the bright moon dropped.

What fond and wayward thoughts will slide
Into a Lover's head!
'O mercy!' to myself I cried,
'If Lucy should be dead!'

(ii)

She dwelt among the untrodden ways
Beside the springs of Dove,
A Maid whom there were none to praise
And very few to love:

A violet by a mossy stone
Half hidden from the eye!
– Fair as a star, when only one
Is shining in the sky.

She lived unknown, and few could know
When Lucy ceased to be;
But she is in her grave, and, oh,
The difference to me!


(iii)

I travelled among unknown men,
In lands beyond the sea;
Nor, England! Did I know till then
What love I bore to thee.

'Tis past, that melancholy dream!
Nor will I quit thy shore
A second time; for still I seem
To love thee more and more.

Among thy mountains did I feel
The joy of my desire;
And she I cherished turned her wheel
Beside an English fire.

Thy mornings showed, thy nights concealed,
The bowers where Lucy played;
And thine too is the last green field
That Lucy's eyes surveyed.

(iv)

Three years she grew in sun and shower,
Then Nature said, 'A lovelier flower
On earth was never sown;
This Child I to myself will take;
She shall be mine, and I will make
A Lady of my own.

'Myself will to my darling be
Both law and impulse: and with me
The Girl, in rock and plain,
In earth and heaven, in glade and bower,
Shall feel an overseeing power
To kindle or restrain.

**glade:** clearing in a wood
**bower:** a shady place

'She shall be sportive as the fawn
That wild with glee across the lawn
Or up the mountain springs;
And her's shall be the breathing balm,
And her's the silence and the calm
Of mute insensate things.

**sportive:** playful
**glee:** delight

'The floating clouds their state shall lend
To her; for her the willow bend;
Nor shall she fail to see
Even in the motions of the Storm
Grace that shall mould the Maiden's form
By silent sympathy.

**insensate:** without
feelings

'The stars of midnight shall be dear
To her; and she shall lean her ear
In many a secret place
Where rivulets dance their wayward round,
And beauty born of murmuring sound
Shall pass into her face.
'And vital feelings of delight
Shall rear her form to stately height,
Her virgin bosom swell;
Such thoughts to Lucy I will give
While she and I together live
Here in this happy dell.'

**rivulets:** streams

Thus Nature spake – The work was done –
How soon my Lucy's race was run!
She died, and left to me
This heath, this calm, and quiet scene;
The memory of what has been,
And never more will be.

(v)
A slumber did my spirit seal;
I had no human fears:
She seemed a thing that could not feel
The touch of earthly years.

No motion has she now, no force;
She neither hears nor sees;
Rolled round in earth's diurnal course,
With rocks, and stones, and trees.

**diurnal:** daily

## FOURTH ASSIGNMENT

**Choose one: one hour**

◆ Discuss and/or write a study of the ways these poems work on the reader. Do you think these are similar to or very different from the way 'Lucy Gray' works? Why? Refer to details from all six poems in your essay. Some things you may wish to compare are:
- the tone of voice you hear in each piece
- the standpoint of the speaker
- the kinds of images Wordsworth uses in each poem
- each poem's structure
- the effect of rhyme at particular moments.

◆ Working alone or in groups, make a storyboard for one of these pieces. Present it to the class, explaining how you went about devising your storyboard.

◆ Individually or in groups, experiment with different ways of performing these five poems.

# *Andrei Voznesensky* | *FIRST FROST/FIRST ICE*

## THINKING/TALKING POINTS

- If there are sounds that some people can hear and others cannot, smells which one nose can detect which others cannot, and if it's true that some people's idea of what is blue or red is different from what other people understand by those words, how far do you think it is possible for any two people to have the same experience?

- Discuss how much you think the language(s) you know affects what you think, understand, see and hear. Would a story you have read be the same story if you retold it in language a five year-old could understand? Why?

- What do you understand by the word 'translation'? Describe to each other some translations you know. Talk about how the translation is similar to/different from the original version.

- One kind of translation is when a work produced in one medium is re-presented in another. For example, Shakespeare's play *Romeo and Juliet* has been re-presented in many different ways: as a ballet, as a song, as an opera, as a novel, as an animation, as a film.

  Talk about some of the things which might happen when a work is translated from, say, a novel into a play or a film. Talk about a film version that you have seen of a book you have read. Discuss some of the ways in which *seeing* a film of a work is different from reading it.

- Another kind of translation is when a work written in one language is re-presented in another.

  Imagine that you are writing a prose piece or a poem on a winter scene. You are looking out of the window. It clouds over and white flakes begin to flutter down from the clouds.

  Now imagine that a Russian student is looking out at a similar winter scene. Do you think both of you would see the same thing? In what ways do you think the Russian prose piece or poem might be different?

# ПЕРВЫЙ ЛЕД

Мерзнет девочка в автомате,
Прячет в зябкое пальтецо
Все в слезах и губной помаде
Перемазанное лицо.

Дышит в худенькие ладошки.
Пальцы — льдышки. В ушах — сережки.

Ей обратно одной, одной
Вдоль по улочке ледяной.

Первый лед. Это в первый раз.
Первый лед телефонных фраз.

Мерзлый след на щеках блестит —
Первый лед от людских обид.

1959

### FIRST ASSIGNMENT

Thirty minutes

◆ Write a two hundred word account of what has been going on in your group for the last thirty minutes.

Compare what each of you has written. Discuss how far you have described the same experience.

### SECOND ASSIGNMENT

Choose one: one hour

◆ On page 154 is a poem. On page 155 is another. Turn to *one* of them. Read it through carefully a few times, then follow these instructions.

The story in the poem you have read is presented in the third person ('A girl ... her ... she ...'). Your job is to translate the poem into a short story of between two hundred and fifty and a thousand words. Present your piece in the first person ('I ... me ... my ...'), choosing one of the two options below.

◆ Imagine you are the girl. It is midnight. In your diary you are writing about what took place this afternoon in the telephone booth and immediately afterwards.

Add details to the few we are given in the poem: sights, sounds, feelings – perhaps the words of that telephone conversation. Try to include nothing in your story which does not fit with what is in the poem you read.

Redraft your piece until you are satisfied with it.

◆ Imagine you are the person the girl was speaking to on the telephone. It is midnight. You are describing to a close friend what took place this afternoon when you answered the girl's telephone call.

Add ideas of your own. Try to include nothing in your story which does not fit with what is in the poem you read.

Redraft your piece until you are satisfied with it.

### PLENARY

Two hours

• Listen to each other's story versions of the poem. Discuss how far each of you has described similar experience(s).

What do you think explains the differences between your stories?

## THIRD ASSIGNMENT

In pairs: one hour

◆ You are the editors of a poetry journal. You have asked four fluent English/Russian speakers to provide an English version of the poem 'First Frost/First Ice' by Andrei Voznesensky.

Four versions have arrived. You will find them on pages 154 to 157. You must decide which one to publish. Alternatively, you may choose to create a new version of the poem which you think is more effective than any of the four you have received.

Describe and justify your decision.

If you create a new 'translation', provide your version and explain why you have written it as you have.

## PLENARY

• Discuss each pair's choice and read out any new versions which were produced. Discuss what you feel this exercise has taught you about translation.

## EXTENSION ASSIGNMENT: COMPARING TRANSLATIONS

Write a critical study, comparing the four translations of Voznesensky's poem. Examine the language of each one carefully and discuss how far you think it is true that these translations provide four completely different poems.

*Marlowe* | *THE PASSIONATE SHEEPHEARD TO HIS LOUE*

*Ralegh* | *A NYMPH'S REPLY TO THE SHEPHERD*

*C Day-Lewis* | *COME LIVE WITH ME AND BE MY LOVE*

One time, however, we were near quarrelling. He said the pleasantest manner of spending a hot July day was lying from morning till evening on a bank of heath in the middle of the moors, with the bees humming dreamily about among the bloom, and the larks singing high up overhead, and the blue sky and bright sun shining steadily and cloudlessly. That was his most perfect idea of heaven's happiness.

Mine was rocking in a rustling green tree, with a west wind blowing, and bright white clouds flitting rapidly above, and not only larks, but throstles, and blackbirds, and linnets, and cuckoos pouring out music on every side, and the moors seen at a distance, broken into cool, dusky dells, but close by great swells of long grass undulating in waves to the breeze, and woods and sounding water, and the whole world awake and wild with joy.

He wanted all to lie in an ecstasy of peace; I wanted all to sparkle and dance in a glorious jubilee. I said his heaven would be only half alive, and he said mine would be drunk; I said I should fall asleep in his, and he said he could not breathe in mine, and began to grow very snappish.

At last we agreed to try both, as soon as the right weather came; and then we kissed each other and were friends.

## THINKING/TALKING POINTS

- Without looking back at the text, see if you can describe in your own way how the two people in this story imagine their ideal places.

- Look back at the text. Which picture of heaven do you find more appealing? Why?

- What impression of these two characters does the passage give you? Which images do you feel suggest their personalities most vividly?

- Later in the story, the two get married. How do you imagine their life together?

- This extract comes from a famous novel first published in 1847. See if you can find out which novel it's from.

**FIRST ASSIGNMENT**

One hour

◆ Write a series of diary entries in which one of these characters describes his/her changing feelings about the relationship, before and after the wedding. What happened on the honeymoon? Has marriage altered the way s/he feels? What's his/her idea of heaven now?

Use the kind of words, images and tone and the style of handwriting/presentation which you feel best brings out the writer's personality and outlook.

# The Passionate Sheepheard to his Loue

### THINKING/TALKING POINTS

• If somebody asked for your idea of heaven, what would it be like? For example, would you think of any of these things:

unwinding

brown    white    purple    blue

a tree-house    being lazy    tranquillity

being full of ideas    the hum of computers

scientific experiments    a riot of wild flowers

a penthouse flat    an inaccessible cave

green    red    yellow    endless variety

talking    isolation    sharing

wine    silence    ambition

manicured lawns

long sandy empty beaches

spring, summer, autumn or winter

a bustling twenty-four hour supermarket

bird song

making things    clocks

messages    energy    fast food

a yacht    being frustrated    security

surprises    love    sex    explosions

warmth    music    cakes    honey

an island    taking

giving

• If somebody asked you to write a piece about paradise, or to paint it, what are some of the images you would include? What would be the tone, the flavour, the colour of your piece?

In a Valentine's greeting, the lover sets out a stall, sings like a blackbird about what s/he has to offer a likely mate. See what you make of this:

# The Passionate Sheepheard to his Loue

**proue:** try out, test

Come liue with mee, and be my loue,
And we will all the pleasures proue,
That Vallies, groues, hills and fieldes,
Woods, or steepie mountaine yeeldes.

And wee will sit vpon the Rocks,
Seeing the Sheepheards feede theyr flocks,
By shallow Riuers, to whose falls,
Melodious byrds sings Madrigalls.

And I will make thee beds of Roses,
And a thousand fragrant poesies,
A cap of flowers, and a kirtle,
Imbroydred all with leaues of Mirtle.

A gowne made of the finest wooll,
Which from our pretty Lambes we pull,
Fayre lined slippers for the cold:
With buckles of the purest gold.

A belt of straw, and Iuie buds,
With Corall clasps and Amber studs,
And if these pleasures may thee moue,
Come liue with mee and be my loue.

The Sheepheards Swaines shall daunce and sing,
For thy delight each May-morning,
If these delights thy mind may moue;
Then liue with mee, and be my loue

## THINKING/TALKING POINTS

- What impression of country life comes across to you here? How is it similar to/different from what you know/imagine life in the countryside to be like?

- What aspects of the shepherd's life does this poem stress? What aspects are overlooked?

## SECOND ASSIGNMENT

One hour: choose one

◆ Design a Valentine's card. Use Marlowe's poem as the text.

◆ Imagine you've received this poem from an admirer.
Write your reply, in verse or prose.

◆ Compose your own version of Marlowe's poem. It may be serious or funny.

Use Marlowe's rhyme scheme and rhythm. Try to use exactly the same number of stanzas too. Instead of the images and the diction he uses, substitute modern ones. For example, instead of being a shepherd, your speaker might be:

| | | | |
|---|---|---|---|
| a scientist | a fire-fighter | a magician | an astronaut |
| a crook | a cleaner | a teacher | a television chef |
| a trainspotter | a dancer | an ecologist | an undertaker |
| a librarian | a musician | a lorry-driver | an accountant |
| a ghost | a doctor | a rock star | a traffic-warden |
| a banker | a traveller | an acrobat | a hairdresser |
| an alien | a junkie | a vampire | a royal |
| a hot-air balloon enthusiast | | someone working in a sweetshop | |
| *The Big Issue* vendor | | | |

Listen to or read these two poems a few times.

# A Nymph's Reply to the Shepherd

If all the world and love were young,
And truth in every shepherd's tongue,
These pretty pleasures might me move
To live with thee, and be thy love.

Time drives the flocks from field to fold
When rivers rage, and rocks grow cold,
And Philomel becometh dumb;
The rest complains of cares to come.

The flowers do fade, and wanton fields
To wayward winter reckoning yields;
A honey tongue, a heart of gall,
Is fancy's spring, but sorrow's fall.

Thy gowns, thy shoes, thy beds of roses,
Thy cap, thy kirtle, and thy posies,
Soon break, soon winter, soon forgotten:
In folly ripe, in reason rotten.

Thy belt of straw and ivy buds,
Thy coral clasps and amber studs,
All these in me no means can move,
To come to thee, and be thy love.

But could youth last, and love still breed,
Had joys no date, no age no need,
Then these delights my mind might move
To live with thee, and be thy love.

# Come, Live with Me and Be my Love

Come, live with me and be my love,
And we will all the pleasure prove
Of peace and plenty, bed and board,
That chance employment may afford.

I'll handle dainties on the docks
And thou shalt read of summer frocks:
At evening by the sour canals
We'll hope to hear some madrigals.

Care on thy maiden brow shall put
A wreath of wrinkles, and thy foot
Be shod with pain: not silken dress
But toil shall tire thy loveliness.

Hunger shall make thy modest zone
And cheat fond death of all but bone –
If these delights thy mind may move,
Then live with me and be my love.

## PERFORMANCE: *POETRY PLEASE*

◆ Prepare the script of a programme suitable for Radio Four around two performances of the poems by Marlowe, Sir Walter Ralegh and C Day-Lewis, and/or some the class has written.

Begin by rehearsing the reading of the poems, trying to find the best tone of voice, tempo and mood for each one. Decide whether you will use one or several contrasting voices.

Start your broadcast with performances of the poems.
Then present a discussion of the pieces in which the presenter and a panel of poetry buffs describe and comment upon the attitudes of the speakers in each poem. What have they got in common? What makes each poem special, memorable, beautiful, amusing, provocative?
Topics which come up might include:
  – differences in imagery, diction, tone, tempo and mood
  – parody and pastiche
  – the different intentions of the poets
  – what the poems suggest to us about the times in which they were written
  – which of the poems the panel thinks will still be popular in four hundred years' time and why.

Conclude your broadcast with another reading of the poems.

Goya: 'Why?' from *The Disasters of War*

## Kipling | DANNY DEEVER

## Newbolt | HE FELL AMONG THIEVES

### THINKING/TALKING POINTS

In pairs

- The announcement 'Dead Man Walking' is heard on Death Row in certain prisons in the United States. It is made by those leading a condemned prisoner to his execution.

  Discuss how the words make you feel. See if you can explain why they have that effect. For example, do you feel the impact of those three words is different from this statement?
  
      'The execution will now proceed.'
  
  If so, why?

- In England, capital punishment used to be known as 'judicial murder'. What do you think that phrase means? Talk about some of the differences between 'murder', 'judicial murder' and 'execution'.

- Why do you think whenever an execution is carried out, people gather outside the prison?

### PRELIMINARY ASSIGNMENT

◆ For centuries, people have argued about whether judicial murder can ever be justified. Imagine you were preparing a programme for television exploring, once again, the arguments for and against capital punishment. As the director of the programme, your job would be to invite into the studio people who could explain clearly the principal arguments for and against reintroducing the death penalty.

See if you can come up with a list of six reasons certain people might be expected to use to justify capital punishment. Then make a list of six reasons others would put forward for outlawing it from all civilised countries.

To help develop your programme, you might decide to use some accounts, fictional and true, of executions. Discuss any you have read or seen in films and how they affected the way you felt about the case for the death penalty.

In this unit, we explore two poems where someone is executed. In the first, we experience things from the point of view of a company of soldiers forced to watch whilst a criminal is hung. In the second, we share the thoughts of the condemned on the night before his death.

Before you work on the poems, talk about how you expect the two pieces to work on the thoughts and feelings of the audience.

### POETRY IN PERFORMANCE

*In groups: one hour*

- Here's a poem written about a hundred years ago. Read it through silently a couple of times. Then read the poem around the group, taking a sentence each in turn.

- Repeat the process until you feel you have a sense of the poem's mood, pace and the characters of the different speakers.

## Danny Deever

'What are the bugles blowin' for?' said Files-on-Parade.
'To turn you out, to turn you out,' the Colour-Sergeant said.
'What makes you look so white, so white?' said Files-on-Parade.
'I'm dreadin' what I've got to watch,' the Colour-Sergeant said.
For they're hangin' Danny Deever, you can hear the Dead March play,
The Regiment's in 'ollow square – they're hangin' him to-day;
They've taken of his buttons off an' cut his stripes away,
An' they're hangin' Danny Deever in the mornin'.

'What makes the rear-rank breathe so 'ard?' said Files-on-Parade.
'It's bitter cold, it's bitter cold,' the Colour-Sergeant said.
'What makes that front-rank man fall down?' said Files-on-Parade.
'A touch o' sun, a touch o' sun,' the Colour-Sergeant said.
They are hangin' Danny Deever, they are marchin' of 'im round,
They 'ave 'alted Danny Deever by 'is coffin on the ground;
An' 'e'll swing in 'arf a minute for a sneakin' shootin' hound –
O they're hangin' Danny Deever in the mornin'!

''Is cot was right-'and cot to mine,' said Files-on-Parade.
''E's sleepin' out an' far to-night,' the Colour-Sergeant said.
'I've drunk 'is beer a score o' times,' said Files-on-Parade.
''E's drinkin' bitter beer alone,' the Colour-Sergeant said.
They are hangin' Danny Deever, you must mark 'im to 'is place,

For 'e shot a comrade sleepin' – you must look 'im in the face;
Nine 'undred of 'is county an' the Regiment's disgrace,
While they're hangin' Danny Deever in the mornin'.

'What's that so black agin the sun?' said Files-on-Parade.
'It's Danny fightin' 'ard for life,' the Colour-Sergeant said.
'What's that that whimpers over 'ead?' said Files-on-Parade.
'It's Danny's soul that's passin' now,' the Colour-Sergeant said.
For they're done with Danny Deever, you can 'ear the quickstep play,
The Regiment's in column, an' they're marchin' us away;
Ho! the young recruits are shakin', an' they'll want their beer to-day,
After hangin' Danny Deever in the mornin'!

## DEVELOPING YOUR PERFORMANCE

- Discuss various ways this poem could be presented to an audience of twelve-year olds. Talk about how you would want them to feel about Danny Deever, about the Colour-Sergeant and about the ordinary soldiers as they witness Danny's execution.

- What do you think would be the best way of presenting the piece?

   Would some people act as Danny and his executioners or would that part of the action take place 'off stage'?

   Would several voices speak together as Files-on-Parade or would you give different bits to different speakers?

   How would the performance begin and end? What music and/or stage action would you add to the simple story Kipling has written?

   Would you include any characters not mentioned in the poem? How would that change the impact of the piece?

- Experiment with ways of presenting the poem and then perform it to the other groups. Talk about the various ways you have re-presented Kipling's poem.

# He Fell Among Thieves

'Ye have robbed,' said he, 'ye have slaughtered and made an end,
Take your ill-got plunder, and bury the dead:
What will ye more of your guest and sometime friend?'
'Blood for our blood,' they said.

He laughed: 'If one may settle the score for five,
I am ready; but let the reckoning stand till day:
I have loved the sunlight as dearly as any alive.'
'You shall die at dawn,' said they.

He flung his empty revolver down the slope,
He climbed alone to the Eastward edge of the trees;
All night long in a dream untroubled of hope
He brooded, clasping his knees.

He did not hear the monotonous roar that fills
The ravine where the Yassin river sullenly flows;
He did not see the starlight on the Laspur hills,
Or the far Afghan snows.

He saw the April noon on his books aglow,
The wistaria trailing in at the window wide;
He heard his father's voice from the terrace below
Calling him down to ride.

He saw the gray little church across the park,
The mounds that hide the loved and honoured dead;
The Norman arch, the chancel softly dark,
The brasses black and red.

He saw the School Close, sunny and green,
The runner beside him, the stand by the parapet wall,
The distant tape, and the crowd roaring between
His own name over all.

He saw the dark wainscot and timbered roof,
The long tables, and the faces merry and keen;
The College Eight and their trainer dining aloof,
The Dons on the dais serene.

He watched the liner's stem ploughing the foam,
He felt her trembling speed and the thrash of her screw;
He heard her passengers' voices talking of home,
He saw the flag she flew.

And now it was dawn. He rose strong on his feet,
And strode to his ruined camp below the wood;
He drank the breath of the morning cool and sweet;
His murderers round him stood

Light on the Laspur hills was broadening fast,
The blood-red snow-peaks chilled to a dazzling white:
He turned, and saw the golden circle at last,
Cut by the Eastern height.

'O glorious Life, Who dwellest in earth and sun,
I have lived, I praise and adore Thee.'
A sword swept.
Over the pass the voices one by one
Faded, and the hill slept.

## SECOND ASSIGNMENT

In pairs

◆ Prepare your own version of the story you have just heard to tell to a group of twelve-year olds. You may decide to present it as a poem, as a short story or as a play.
   Don't worry if there are details in the story you cannot remember or would like to change. Concentrate upon these things:
   – the situation the main character finds him/herself in
   – the location you imagine for the story
   – the sort of people who are in control
   – the kinds of things the main character thinks about during the night
   – the way the story ends: the mood the audience is left in.

## THIRD ASSIGNMENT

◆ The night before the morning after ...
   What situations might someone find themselves in when s/he is certain that the next night will be his/her last?
   Choose one of those situations to write about.

   You may decide to write it in the first person, beginning something like this:

Prison Camp P007/1    April 14th    2 am

Just three hours to go. I'm not nervous any more: suddenly my mind is clear as crystal. I think about Sam a lot and one of the guards has promised to send my bundle home ...

You could write in the third person, beginning rather like this:

Chris sat on the bunk, hoping her head would clear, her thoughts start to untangle themselves. How had it happened? Could it be true what they'd told her? Yes, there was no point pretending any more, one thing was certain. By this time tomorrow the world would have to go about its business without her help ...

## EXTENSION ASSIGNMENT: CRITICAL STUDY

Rudyard Kipling who died in 1936 and Sir Henry Newbolt who died in 1938 were, in their day, very popular poets. Their verse was learned by many children at school. You may find people in your family who can recite some of their pieces off by heart.

Today many people find their poetry not just old-fashioned but offensive. Is it possible to say, just from the examples you have studied, what qualities made their verse so popular to earlier generations? What did you like/dislike about the poems in this unit?

Read them through closely again. See if you can detect the aspects of the writing which people might find distasteful now. Think particularly about the presentation of the central characters. What clues do the poems give us about their backgrounds, their education, their social position? What notion of 'manliness' do you feel the poems offer us? How do you feel about those notions? Why?

When you have talked about the two poems and the way they present their material, write an essay in which you argue the case for including one, both or neither of these once popular poems in a new anthology of verse to be called *One Hundred Great English Poems*.

## FURTHER EXPLORATIONS

### Films
*The Crying Game*; *In Cold Blood*; *Dead Man Walking*

### Novels
Truman Capote: *In Cold Blood*
Arthur Koestler: *Darkness at Noon*

*Jenny Joseph* | *DAWN WALKERS*

On your own, then in
pairs: twenty minutes

### THINKING/TALKING POINTS

- Close your eyes. See if you can recall the last time you saw:
    - someone crying in the street
    - a couple having an argument
    - a parent telling off a child in public
    - someone hurt in a fight or in an accident.

- Describe to each other one such incident you remember. Provide as many details as you can recall. For example:
    - where you were when you saw the incident: the time, the place
    - what the weather was like
    - the expressions on people's faces
    - how they were dressed
    - the way they were moving
    - what they were saying
    - what you were feeling as an onlooker.

- Were you there long enough to see how things ended? Or were you left wondering what happened next?

## Dawn Walkers

Anxious eyes loom down the damp-black streets
Pale staring girls who are walking away hard
From beds where love went wrong or died or turned away,
Treading their misery beneath another day
Stamping to work into another morning.

In all our youths there must have been some time
When the cold dark has stiffened up the wind
But suddenly, like a sail stiffening with wind,
Carried the vessel on, stretching the ropes, glad of it.

But listen to this now: this I saw one morning
I saw a young man running, for a bus I thought,

Needing to catch it on this murky morning
Dodging the people crowding to work or shopping early.
And all heads stopped and turned to see how he ran
To see would he make it, the beautiful strong young man.
Then I noticed a girl running after, calling out 'John'.
He must have left his sandwiches I thought.
But she screamed 'John wait'. He heard her and ran faster,
Using his muscled legs and studded boots.
We knew she'd never reach him. 'Listen to me John.
Only once more' she cried. 'For the last time, John, please wait,
    please listen.'
He gained the corner in a spurt and she
Sobbing and hopping with her red hair loose
(Made way for by the respectful audience)
Followed on after, but not to catch him now.
Only that there was nothing left to do.

The street closed in and went on with its day.
A worn old man standing in the heat from the baker's
Said 'Surely to God the bastard could have waited'.

## ASSIGNMENT: POEM INTO SHORT STORY

**Choose one:
ninety minutes**

◆ Imagine yourself as one of the characters involved in this story: the girl, the boy or the old man who was watching. Think about how that person would have experienced the events Jenny Joseph's poem describes: what s/he would have seen, heard, felt.

You may decide to begin the story a little earlier than the events described in the poem – and/or to continue a few moments after it ended.

Consider what might have been happening between John and his girlfriend. Had they spent the night together? Had she called round? What led up to John's bursting away? You may wish to include some fragments of their argument in your version of the story.

◆ Every day we encounter people we don't know. Some we see every day yet never speak to: in the street; on the bus; in a shop or looking out of a window. There are other people we may have spent an hour or more observing: in a queue; on a train journey or in the doctor's waiting room.

Try to remember one particular person or group of people that you've observed and speculated about. Jot down as many details as you can remember about them: what they wore; their hairstyles; the way they behaved; your guesses about their occupation, background and lifestyles.

Decide on the dozen or so details you feel suggest most about their personalities. Now read Jenny Joseph's poem again to yourself a few times. Using her piece as a model, write a poem based on your own experiences. See how closely you can follow the structure and style of 'Dawn Walkers'. You may even try to make it exactly the same length – two hundred and sixty words, including the title.

# Seamus Heaney | *MID-TERM BREAK*

## THINKING/TALKING POINTS

In groups of four

Listen to someone who has prepared it read the poem opposite. It is a story written in the first person.

- When you have heard the story read aloud a couple of times, take it in turns to retell it to each other. Listen carefully to how each person retells the story. Some will remember different things from what others recall. Some will develop what the story only gave us hints about.

- When you have listened to each other's versions, discuss what each of you felt was most important in the story. Why did some details seem more interesting or significant to you than they did to other people? Did the story remind you of any similar experiences you have been through?

- Now turn to the text of the story-poem you have heard. Read it through to yourselves a few times. When you feel you've 'got' the story clear in your head, make a note of any details which you had forgotten after the reading, but which now seem important. Are there any details which you think you misunderstood when you listened to the story being read?

- If you were to pick out just four moments from the poem which helped you to feel most of the speaker's experience, which four would they be?

# Mid-Term Break

I sat all morning in the college sick bay
Counting bells knelling classes to a close.
At two o'clock our neighbours drove me home.

In the porch I met my father crying –
He had always taken funerals in his stride –
And Big Jim Evans saying it was a hard blow.

The baby cooed and laughed and rocked the pram
When I came in, and I was embarrassed
By old men standing up to shake my hand

And tell me they were 'sorry for my trouble'.
Whispers informed strangers I was the eldest,
Away at school, as my mother held my hand

In hers and coughed out angry tearless sighs.
At ten o'clock the ambulance arrived
With the corpse, stanched and bandaged by the nurses.

Next morning I went up into the room. Snowdrops
And candles soothed the bedside; I saw him
For the first time in six weeks.  Paler now,

Wearing a poppy bruise on his left temple,
He lay in the four foot box as in his cot.
No gaudy scars, the bumper knocked him clear.

A four foot box, a foot for every year.

## ASSIGNMENT

**Choose one**

If this is a true story, the writer has told us only a few of the many things s/he heard, saw, felt and realised during that 'Mid-Term Break'. If instead of writing a poem, the speaker had been telling a friend or praying or writing a diary entry about what s/he was going through, s/he would probably have treated the experience very differently and described different things.

Choose one of the following situations. Use as much of the original story as you think is necessary but then develop things in whatever way seems to you consistent with the way the speaker wrote the poem.

◆ It is twenty-five years later. The speaker's daughter finds a photograph of a relative she never knew she had. She asks what he was like and what happened to him. She wonders why she has never been told about him.

Write their conversation.

◆ Imagine you are the speaker. It is mid-way through a Maths lesson when you are called from the room by the Deputy Head. Describe the events of ten minutes as if they were happening as you describe them. You might begin something like this:

> 'I've never understood percentages. Probably never will. Look at Chris over there, smug and efficient. Will this lesson ever end?
> Oh no! What's Greeny doing coming into the class? Me? What does Beeny Greeny want with me this time? I'm always the one Greeny picks on. Miserable sod! Looks as if he's lost a quid and found a penny ...'

◆ Imagine you are the speaker sitting on the train chugging back to school. Write about your memories and feelings. What will you always remember about your brother? And about the funeral, and the way people behaved? Do you feel numb, angry, confused or what? Give the reader a sense of both the journeys you are making: in the train and in your head. How is this journey back to school different from the last one you made?

◆ Imagine you were the driver of the car which killed the child. Unobserved, you look through the curtains as the funeral procession passes. Describe your tangle of memories and feelings. Do you know the family? Was the death anyone's fault? Do you expect your life to be different after what's happened? Why?

# Appendices

# First Frost

A girl is freezing in a telephone booth,
huddled in her flimsy coat,
her face stained by tears
and smeared with lipstick.

She breathes on her thin little fingers,
Fingers like ice. Glass beads in her ears.

She has to beat her way back alone
down the icy street.

First frost. A beginning of losses,
The first frost of telephone phrases.

It is the start of winter glittering on her cheek,
the first frost of having been hurt.

Andrei Voznesensky
translated by George Reavey

# First Ice

A girl freezes in a telephone booth,
In her draughty overcoat she hides
A face all smeared
In tears and lipstick.

She breathes on her thin palms,
Her fingers are icy. She wears earrings.

She'll have to go home alone, alone,
Along the icy street.

First ice. It is the first time.
The first ice of telephone phrases.

Frozen tears glitter on her cheeks –
The first ice of human hurt.

Andrei Voznesensky
translated by Stanley Kunitz

# First Ice

A girl in a phone box is freezing cold,
Retreating into her shivery coat.
Her face in too much make-up's smothered
With grubby tearstains and lipstick smudges.

Into her tender palms she's breathing.
Fingers – ice lumps. In earlobes – earrings.

She goes back home, alone, alone,
Behind her the frozen telephone.

First ice. The very first time.
First ice of a telephone conversation.

On her cheeks tear traces shine –
First ice of human humiliation.

Andrei Voznesensky
translated by Herbert Marshall

# The First Ice

In the telephone box the girl freezes,
her face is smeared with running tears
and lipstick, she huddles, peers
out from her chilly collar, aches –
blows upon her thin little paws –
icicle fingers! Earrings flash.
Back-alone as she is, along
the long lonely, icy lane.
The first ice. The first time, it was
first ice cracking in phoned phrases –
the frozen track shines on her cheeks –
first ice on her insulting ears.

Andrei Voznesensky
translator unknown

Storyboard of stanza from 'The Wreck of the Deutschland' by Polina Bakhnova

# Acknowledgements

The authors and publishers wish to thank the following for permission to use copyright material:

Anvil Press Poetry Ltd for 'In Mrs Tilscher's Class' from *The Other Country* by Carol Ann Duffy, 1990, and 'Room', 'The Captain of the 1964 Top of the Form Team', 'Stafford Afternoons' and 'Litany' from *Mean Time* by Carol Ann Duffy, 1993; Bantam Books, a division of Bantam Doubleday Dell Publishing Group, Inc, for 'First Ice' from *Modern European Poetry*, edited by Willis Barnstone. Copyright © 1966 by Bantam Books, a division of Bantam Doubleday Dell Publishing Group, Inc; Basic Books, a subsidiary of Perseus Books Group, LLC, for 'First Ice', trans. Stanley Kunitz from Andrei Voznesensky, *Antiworlds and the Fifth Ace: Poetry*, eds Patricia Blake and Max Hayward. Copyright © 1966, 1967 by Basic Books, Inc, copyright © 1963 by Encounter Ltd; Sheila Colman, on behalf of The Lord Alfred Douglas Literary Estate, for 'London' by Lord Alfred Douglas; English and Media Centre for 'View from the Window' by David Green from *City Lines*, 1982; Faber and Faber Ltd for 'Mid-Term Break' from *New Selected Poems 1966–1987* by Seamus Heaney; and extracts from 'The Howling of Wolves' from *Wodwo* by Ted Hughes, *The Wasteland* from *Collected Poems 1909–1962* by T S Eliot, and *War Music* by Christopher Logue; Heinemann Educational Publishers, a division of Reed Educational & Professional Publishing Ltd, for an extract from 'Sir Gawain and the Grene Gome' by R T Jones, 1972; David Higham Associates on behalf of the Estate of the author for an extract from *Under Milk Wood* by Dylan Thomas, J M Dent; John Johnson Ltd on behalf of the author for 'Dawn Walkers' from *Selected Poems* by Jenny Joseph, Bloodaxe, 1992; Peter Newbolt for 'He Fell Among Thieves' from *Selected Poems of Henry Newbolt*, Hodder & Stoughton, 1981; Random House UK on behalf of the Estate of the author for 'Come Live With Me and Be my Love' from *The Complete Poems* by C Day-Lewis, Sinclair-Stevenson, 1992. Copyright © 1992 in this edition, The Estate of C Day-Lewis; and on behalf of the author for an extract from *The Child in Time* by Ian McEwan, Jonathan Cape; Routledge for 'First Ice' from Voznesensky Selected Poems, trans. Herbert Marshall, Methuen, 1966; A P Watt on behalf of The National Trust for 'Danny Deever' by Rudyard Kipling.

Thanks are also due to the following for permission to reproduce photographs:
'The Misses Tracy-Travell' by Dance [or Holland], Nathaniel (1734-1811), Agnew & Sons, London, p 119 (above), also 'Wait for Me! (Returning Home from School)' by Anderson, Sophie (1823-1903), Christopher Wood Gallery, London, p 119 (below), UK/Bridgeman Art Library, London/New York; Palace/NFFC/ITC (Courtesy Kobal), p 68; Popperfoto/Ingram, p 140 (above); The Ronald Grant Archive, p 52; SOLO (Daily Mail)/Bill Cross, p 89 (above); Telegraph Colour Library, p 88; Tony Stone Images, p 89 (below).

Illustrations: G J Galsworthy p 12; Judy Stevens pp 19, 130; Polina Bakhnova p 158.

Every effort has been made to reach copyright holders; the publishers would like to hear from anyone whose rights they have unknowingly infringed.